Blaming the Poor

DISCARD

Blaming the Poor

· ·

The Long Shadow of the Moynihan Report on Cruel Images about Poverty

SUSAN D. GREENBAUM

Rutgers University Press

New Brunswick, NJ, and London

Library of Congress Cataloging-in-Publication Data
    Greenbaum, Susan D.
    Blaming the poor: the long shadow of the Moynihan report on cruel images about poverty
/ Susan D. Greenbaum.
        pages cm
    Includes bibliographical references and index.
    ISBN 978-0-8135-7414-1 (hardback)—ISBN 978-0-8135-7413-4 (pbk.)—ISBN
978-0-8135-7416-5 (e-book (web pdf))
    1. United States. Department of Labor. Office of Policy Planning and Research. Negro
family, the case for national action. 2. Poor African Americans—Social conditions. 3. African
American families—Social conditions. 4. African Americans—Public opinion. 5. Poverty—
United States—History. 6. Public welfare—United States—History. 7. United States—Race
relations—History. 8. United States—Social policy. 9. Moynihan, Daniel P. (Daniel Patrick),
1927–2003. I. Title.

    E185.86.U52G74 2015
    362.5089'96073—dc23
    2014041363A

British Cataloging-in-Publication record for this book is available from the British Library.

Visit our website: http://rutgerspress.rutgers.edu

Manufactured in the United States of America

Contents

Preface

As a total coincidence, my first job after earning a BA in Sociology was for Daniel Patrick Moynihan. I was a temporary interviewer at the Joint Center for Urban Studies in Cambridge, Massachusetts. Following a strict protocol, I was gathering data for some kind of study that involved bothering white suburban households during, or just after, their dinners to question them about their opinions on various topics, including family values. It was 1968. Moynihan was then director of the Joint Center and nominally the head of everything going on there at the time. My team of interviewers met him once, when he came down to our basement quarters to say hello. He was quite congenial—a large, red-faced man wearing what looked like a very expensive suit.

At the time, I was only vaguely aware of the swirl of controversy about the report. I was glad to have the job, although in the end it became part of the argument I waged with myself about why it would be better to become an anthropologist, which anthropology finally won. I have been interested in poverty and race for nearly a half century, and I have been advocating for honestly collaborative community-based applied research for nearly that long. Negative stereotypes about poor mothers, fathers, and teens, especially those who are African American, are omnipresent across a fairly wide political spectrum, and these images cripple thinking about how to alleviate these inequities. Recurrent debates since the 1964 launch of the War on Poverty tread the same old ground, and support for punishment and vilification of poor people ebbs and flows depending on the politics of the moment. The present trends seem to favor vilification, which is one of the reasons I wrote this book. On the verge of the Fiftieth Anniversary of the Moynihan Report, when the ideas he made respectable are back with gusto, I hope to provoke critical understanding of what I argue are misbegotten beliefs.

Many people contributed to this book. My husband, Paul, is as always my best critic, followed soon after by my daughter Rosa, both of whom offered valuable feedback and encouragement. My friends and colleagues Donileen Loseke and Marilyn Williams offered thoughtful advice, as did Paul Gorski, Steve Steinberg, and Carol Stack. My former students Lance Arney and Beverly Ward have been important influences. I am particularly grateful to Herbert Gans, whose communications at various stages have been very helpful. And, thanks to Stevo, Jane, Ivory, Orrin, Juan, Evelia, Bob, Herman, Manuel, Graciela, Sylvia, both Franciscos, Taft, Harold, Wesley, Marlo, Shannon, Vann, Chloe, Otis, and dozens of other people whose friendship has enlightened and enlivened my work.

Blaming the Poor

1

Introduction

● ● ● ● ● ● ● ● ● ● ● ● ● ● ● ● ● ●

> From the wild Irish slums of the 19th century
> eastern seaboard, to the riot-torn suburbs of
> Los Angeles, there is one unmistakable lesson
> in American history; a community that allows
> a large number of men to grow up in broken
> families, dominated by women, never acquiring
> any stable relationship to male authority, never
> acquiring any set of rational expectations about
> the future—that community asks for and gets
> chaos. Crime, violence, unrest, disorder—most
> particularly the furious, unrestrained lashing
> out at the whole social structure—that is not
> only to be expected; it is very near to inevitable.
> And it is richly deserved.
> —D. P. Moynihan, "A Family Policy for the
> Nation," *America*, Sept. 18, 1965

On August 11, 1965, the predominantly African American Watts neighborhood in Los Angeles exploded in violence that lasted three days, claiming thirty-four lives and injuring more than one thousand people.

1

Coincidentally, a publication of the US Department of Labor report titled *The Negro Family: The Case for National Action* had just been leaked to the press.[1] Written by Daniel Patrick Moynihan, then a thirty-nine-year-old assistant secretary for policy planning and research in the Department of Labor, the report set off a flurry of news articles that blamed the violence in Watts on defects in African American families and culture. Moynihan's contribution to the debate on civil rights, race, and poverty came at a very pregnant moment—on the exact date that the Voting Rights Act was finally passed, and in the wake of a fateful decision to greatly expand the War in Vietnam at the expense of the War on Poverty. This report and the debate it ignited arguably helped alter the direction of social justice in the United States, not in a good way.

This book examines the regrettably durable impact of Moynihan's legacy for race relations and social policy in the US, with an emphasis on the humiliating image the report cast of poor black families and the misleading explanation for where poverty comes from. In particular, the "tangle of pathology" that Moynihan alluded to in the above quotation, and spelled out at length in his report, still is considered by many politicians and policy researchers to be the root cause of poverty. This idea redirects blame for substandard schools, low wages, and scarcity of jobs away from the structural forces that caused these problems while simultaneously reinforcing stereotypes about African American families. His association between female-headed families and violent black males seemingly confirmed the widespread belief that black men are raised to be dangerous.

In early 1964 President Lyndon Johnson had fully embraced the Civil Rights movement and declared war on poverty in the United States. The Office of Economic Opportunity (OEO) was created in August 1964, one month after passage of the landmark Civil Rights Act. A raft of important new social programs—Head Start, Medicare, Medicaid, Legal Services—had been put into place. In the background, however, the guns of war were growing louder, and a succession of black urban uprisings were threatening popular support for the Civil Rights movement. Moynihan's report reflected the liberal end of a growing backlash against increasingly belligerent protest and unease with a revolution against traditional thinking about racial differences and the alleged deficiencies of poor people. Framed as a policy document to help uplift poor black families and correct the effects of past discrimination, it came to be regarded by both supporters and detractors as an indictment of African American culture, a pessimistic warning that legal rights and safety net programs would not be enough.

The report was seventy-eight pages of somewhat unconventional prose and a blizzard of charts, tables, and graphs. It was assembled fairly hastily in the winter and early spring of 1965. The introduction recounted in florid language the moral case for African American equality contrasted with the political realities of racist resistance. In the preface, the author explained that despite political progress, the economic condition of black people in the United States was actually getting worse. He then got right to the heart of his argument: "The fundamental problem . . . is that of family structure. The evidence—not final, but powerfully persuasive—is that the Negro family in the urban ghettos is crumbling. . . . So long as this situation persists, the cycle of poverty and disadvantage will continue to repeat itself."

It was unguarded language for a government report and a peculiar topic to come from the Labor Department, which was nominally in charge of employment, not family well-being. There was indirect attention to the problems of employment discrimination and the high rate of black male unemployment, but this was presented within the context of what were described as fragile families. The connection between joblessness and black family dissolution was demonstrated with reference to writing by the black sociologist E. Franklin Frazier about adjustment problems of southern migrants in northern cities, supplemented with census data on the correspondence between rates of unemployment and divorce and other correlated conditions. Although Moynihan did assert that joblessness was the major problem facing African Americans, his focus was not on measures to expand employment, but on the psychological effects of male unemployment. A man without a job was not a breadwinner, and his masculinity was undermined by the inability to fulfill that vital role. That conundrum sowed the seed of what he labeled a tangle of pathology, encapsulating all the alleged ills of lower-class African American culture—teen pregnancy, unmarried parenthood, absent fathers, "matriarchal" dominance of family life, educational failure, juvenile delinquency, and adult crime.[2] Boys raised in such families set their feet early on a path to failure as workers and as fathers, in a cycle that continued across generations.

Moynihan described these conditions as a self-perpetuating force that was immune to normal social intervention. Although he conceded that correlations between female-headed families and poverty, "illegitimacy," crime, school dropout rates, and other social problems could not distinguish cause from effect, he claimed he had found a single statistic that made his case. During the early years of the 1960s, black male unemployment declined and welfare enrollment by black women increased. Popularly known as "Moynihan's scissors," this inverse correlation was deemed to offer proof that jobs alone would not cure dependency on welfare. He claimed that this discovery established that self-perpetuation of poverty already had taken hold.[3] Thus his conviction that the only path to true equality lay in somehow fixing the deficient family structure of African Americans. "Three centuries of injustice have brought about deep-seated structural dislocations in the life of the Negro American. At this point, the present tangle of pathology is capable of perpetuating itself without assistance from the white world."[4]

Moynihan attributed what he called "matriarchal" tendencies among African Americans to the legacy of slavery and Jim Crow discrimination. A long history, possibly even traceable to Africa, was responsible for this flaw in the social structure of African Americans and was most prevalent among those who were poor. Some had managed to assimilate conventional values favoring nuclear families, and they formed the emerging black middle class; but for the struggling masses, poverty and family "disorganization" were destined to be entwined. Unlike other minorities who suffered from discrimination, such as Jews who were ultimately able to find success in the American economy, African Americans appeared to be doomed to failure by internal flaws in their ethnic social structure.

The background and context of Moynihan's thinking about these matters is important. He was not trained as a social scientist or a researcher. Although he had finished college and earned an MA, it was many years earlier (1949). He had begun, but long postponed, work on a PhD. His entree into academics came by way of his involvement with the political career of Averell Harriman, then governor of New York. When Harriman lost his bid for reelection in 1958, Moynihan was commissioned to write the history of his administration, which included a faculty position at Syracuse University. While there he completed his PhD in International Relations from Tufts in 1961. His dissertation concerned international labor organizations. This topic later formed the basis for his appointment in 1963 in the Department of Labor, during the Kennedy administration, on whose campaign he had worked. Moynihan was a prolific writer who authored a series of magazine articles for the *Reporter*, edited by Irving Kristol. The *Reporter* was a widely circulated, mostly liberal, publication. Moynihan's articles about transportation and automobile safety brought both praise and notice. Kristol, who several years later would become disenchanted with liberal ideas and ultimately come to be known as the "godfather of neoconservatism," introduced him to Nathan Glazer, a well-known sociologist who was writing a book about ethnicity in New York.

Glazer commissioned Moynihan to write a chapter on the Irish, and he also wrote much of the conclusion, earning credit as second author.[5] *Beyond the Melting Pot* drew instant acclaim. It won the 1964 Anisfeld-Wolf Award in Race Relations and was trumpeted as a new direction in the study of race and ethnicity. The book contained chapters on each of the major ethnic groups in New York City—"the Negroes, Puerto Ricans, Jews, Italians, and Irish." It was designed both to describe and compare the origins and accomplishments of these various groups. Glazer wrote all the group chapters, except for the one on the Irish, and Moynihan wrote most of the final chapter. The substance of the descriptions was about culture and history, and the varying achievements of groups who shared the same political and geographic landscape. Comparisons were drawn that can only be described as invidious. The authors offered a modified apology for what they feared might be regarded as "harsh" judgments, and wrote, "we ask understanding of those who will be offended."[6] Although this book was widely cited and praised when it came out, it has not weathered the test of time. The chapters on African Americans and Puerto Ricans are mainly negative, containing assertions that were arguable at the time, and are even more contentious in light of contemporary scholarship. Family structure and educational attainment were major themes and points of comparison; Puerto Ricans and African Americans were found wanting in both aspects.

Involvement with this project established Moynihan's credentials as an expert on race and urban problems, and his association with Glazer, whose chapter on "Negroes" strongly emphasized female-headed families and "broken homes," surely helped shape Moynihan's perspective on these issues. In April 1964, shortly after *Beyond the Melting Pot* came out, Moynihan was invited to attend a conference sponsored by the American Academy of Arts and Sciences to plan a major study titled "The Negro in America." He was one of seventeen scholars at this initial event to define the research agenda, not one of whom was black.[7] As part of the Department of Labor, Moynihan emphasized the problems of unemployment and offered the idea that African Americans should receive special treatment by the government in overcoming the obstacles they faced in securing adequate jobs and wages. This suggestion failed to resonate with others in attendance, many of whom feared it might stir a backlash or appear patronizing. An unnamed professor offered the following concern: "Thus we could be presented as the white liberals of the American Academy who are engaged in rationalizing not the status quo, but the future status [quo]." The white liberals in attendance, however, were not shy about discussing problems of black families that presumably led to assorted collective failures. This incident was cited by Lee Rainwater and William Yancey in their compendium on the Moynihan Report and the controversy surrounding it, where they also surmised that this conference, following so soon after Moynihan's involvement with the *Melting Pot*, reinforced his emergent assessment that family structure was the central problem hindering African American progress. They added that Moynihan himself had grown up in a fatherless household, speculating that he could personally relate to problems caused by this condition.[8]

Such was the atmosphere surrounding the initiation of the report Moynihan designed the following winter, a turbulent time when President Kennedy had been assassinated and his successor (LBJ) was promising an aggressive stance on equal rights and economic justice. Two factors in the public imagination, and the halls of academia, during that period heightened attention to the role of family structure in explaining poverty.

First was a controversy already in motion over the "culture of poverty." Oscar Lewis, a well-known Marxist anthropologist, had published articles and monographs about Mexican peasants and impoverished Puerto Ricans that described distinctive beliefs, customs, and values he said were nurtured by poverty and passed from parents to children in the same fashion as more functional types of enculturation among other classes. Michael Harrington's very popular book on stubborn pockets of poverty in the midst of growing prosperity, *The Other America*, picked up on Lewis's slogan and offered a more qualified observation that dysfunctional ways of life in poor communities impeded members from seeking opportunities or envisioning possibilities for self-improvement. The crucible of culture is the family, and the upbringing of poor children was increasingly the focus of explanations for the tenacity of their unfortunate circumstances.[9]

Freudian-influenced psychology was another factor that amplified the importance attached to family structure during this period. Two psychologists at the Academy of Arts and Sciences conference (Erik Erikson and Thomas Pettigrew) articulated the importance of distorted gender roles and developmental factors in explaining what they considered were ineffective black responses to societal prejudice. The notion of the strong father figure as critical to the development of children, especially males, was firmly ensconced in both academic and popular thought of that era. The majority of middle-class wives did not work outside the home, a pattern that was deemed important for the proper socialization of children. Departures from legally married nuclear families with clearly defined gender roles were viewed as deviant and potentially destructive. Additionally, most recognized African American scholars also decried the disparate pattern of female-headed households and nonmarital child rearing in low-income black communities. In addition to Frazier, who was mentioned earlier, Kenneth Clark, St. Clair Drake, and even W.E.B. Du Bois had written about this issue and the problems they attributed to it.[10] So, as the young Pat Moynihan formulated his plan to write a groundbreaking policy study about the cycle of black poverty, he surely felt he was standing on solid ground.

However, when the report came out, initially as a leak to newspaper columnists, it ignited a firestorm. Based largely on the report, *Newsweek* prominently featured a four-page article about troubled black families only days before the outbreak of the August 11 Watts uprising. Less than a week after Watts, the well-connected columnists Roland Evans and Robert Novak wrote a fairly lurid piece about the report in the *Wall Street Journal*, for the first time labeling it the "Moynihan Report." They characterized it as "the much-suppressed, much leaked Labor Department document which strips away the usual equivocations and exposes the ugly truth about the big-city Negro's plight."[11] According to James Patterson in his 2010 book about the report, in singling out the usually nameless bureaucrat who wrote it (Moynihan's name was in the headline), Evans and Novak made him "something of a household name."[12] They also stated that Moynihan was motivated directly by urban riots: "The report stems from the big city Negro riots last summer [1964]. The violence was deeply disturbing to Daniel P. (Pat) Moynihan, the liberal intellectual and politician who was then Assistant Secretary of Labor (he resigned last month to run for president of the New York City Council)."[13]

Continuing coverage of Watts and an outpouring of commentators' rhetoric about the dangers it revealed further elevated Moynihan's reputation as the author of a supposedly scientific justification for racist ideas about the uprising. Meanwhile, as the article indicated, in what might be construed as a plug, Moynihan had resigned from the Labor Department to run for a seat on the New York City Council. He lost in the primary, however, possibly due to the negative publicity that followed not long after he entered. Although he was not elected, he was offered an academic post at Wesleyan University, where he taught a seminar on "racial issues."

As Moynihan settled into his new faculty post and began a speaking tour based on his presumed expertise as a scholar of racial matters, an explosion of both criticism and praise surrounded him. Through the month of August, news coverage of the report continued to build, always connected to Watts and the notion that African Americans were a pathological group. A popular quote from the report was repeatedly printed in these pieces: "The very essence of the male animal from the bantam rooster to the four-star general is to strut. Indeed, in 19th century America, a particular type of exaggerated male boastfulness became almost a national style. Not for the Negro male. The 'sassy nigger' was lynched."[14] In framing an essential difference between black and white males (without commenting on the violence done to black by white men), Moynihan drew on the work of Stanley Elkins, who theorized that slavery had shaped docile, infantile, and submissive personality patterns in African American males, the "Sambo" complex.[15] These references offered considerable grist for racist interpretations and generated angry responses by civil rights leaders.

Another area of controversy was Moynihan's conclusion that African American women were overeducated and overemployed. He suggested that if black women lost jobs in a program designed to increase black male employment, that would not be bad. Implicitly, the necessity-driven strength of black women emasculated their men-folk. He also suggested that they favored daughters over sons in preparation for school and work.

An issue that got less attention at the time, but was destined for irony, was his idea that more black men should go into the military. He pointed to their poor performance on the IQ tests that were part of qualifying for entry into the armed forces. He argued that more aggressive preparation and relaxed recruitment standards would help solve employment problems and would provide a more masculine and disciplined environment for the undisciplined and overly feminized black male. As he wrote this prescription, General William Westmoreland was successfully arguing for a massive buildup of forces in Vietnam. A large number of African American males did serve in that war, but the effects for those who managed to survive were more often negative than positive.

Critical response was rapid and in many cases vituperative. Researchers and policy experts in and outside of government pointed out problems with Moynihan's logic and his use and interpretation of data. Mary Keyserling, director of the Women's Bureau of the Department of Labor, complained about his implicit attack on black women and the suggestion that they were creating problems by supporting their children. She was especially opposed to any policy suggestions that would sacrifice black women's jobs to create opportunities for black males.[16]

Other criticisms were that his findings were oversimplified, that they were phrased in alarming language not commensurate with the actual data, that he glossed all black families into a single pathological stereotype, and that he failed to control adequately for income and other key variables in the analyses. Academics weighed in, some in apparent complicity with disgruntled public officials, making similar arguments. He was accused of "blaming the victim" in a well-traveled piece in the *Nation* by William Ryan, a Harvard psychologist who later published a book with that title.[17] Civil rights leaders, including Bayard Rustin, James Farmer, and Martin Luther King Jr., also complained about victim blaming and the reinforcement of stereotypes about black men and women. King pointed out that identifying a problem could either lead to a solution or make it worse. He feared the latter, but his treatment of Moynihan was fairly gentle. Not so with Farmer, who lambasted the report for diverting attention from the real problems facing black people and insulting the whole group for those who were too poor to take proper care of their children: "This well-enough intentioned analysis provides fuel for a new racism . . . it succeeds in taking the real tragedy of black poverty and serving it up as an essentially salacious 'discovery' suggesting that Negro mental health should be the first order of business in a civil rights revolution."[18] He and others implied that the government was trying to redefine and expropriate the movement they had built.

Moynihan was reportedly dejected about all of this criticism. Patterson describes it as a low point in his life, "a moment lost," and Godfrey Hodgson's biography describes it as "the dark hour."[19] Rainwater and Yancey's 1967 postmortem on the Moynihan Report defended him as the victim of oversimplified and sensationalist media coverage. They argued that a close reading of the report showed that his real concern was first and always with the huge employment gap that rendered such a large number of African American men unable to provide for their families. They contend that the issue would have been handled much more constructively if the Labor Department had simply reviewed and edited the report before making it public to ensure it was received within the context that had been intended. Alice O'Connor offered a more complex analysis of how such a well-regarded liberal could give birth to such acrimonious racial condemnation. In her excellent book on the evolution and politics of poverty research, she argues that Moynihan adopted a strategy that relied on "using pathology to make a dramatic case for structural reform."[20] Rainwater and Yancey concurred, stating that "Moynihan wanted his statistics to bleed."[21] In other words, he focused on crime, sex, and family values as a means to gain attention for a problem he thought was caused by employment discrimination. If that was his intention, it backfired. The pathology stuck, and the argument about fairness in employment was submerged. Indeed, the alleged pathology of black men became a respectable pretext for not hiring them.

In the years following the initial controversy, academic consensus against theories about black family disorganization and the "culture" of poverty grew stronger. Two works that came out in the 1970s were especially influential. Carol Stack published a widely cited ethnographic study of urban African American family networks in Illinois that belied Moynihan's characterizations of isolated and ineffective female-headed households. Stack's work injected a much-needed anthropological perspective on kinship and family structure and offered convincing evidence that black poverty was the result of discrimination and racism, not internal failures of the African American community.[22] To the contrary, flexible extended kinship ties were a cushion against the worst effects of poverty and deprivation. Unlike Moynihan, who made glancing references to the ill effects of discrimination, Stack demonstrated how exactly it operated in the case of flesh and blood families and individuals. Two years later, in 1976, the historian Herbert Gutman published an extensive study of African American families in slavery and beyond that contradicted Moynihan's assertions about the effects of history on contemporary black family structure.[23] His work indicated that stable two-parent families were predominant until after World War II. The dislocations of deepening rural poverty and challenges of urban migration, much more than the long roots of slavery, were the principal factors that led to sharply increasing numbers of marital breakups and fatherless families.

Stack's conclusions about resilience and gender were at odds with Moynihan's view of black families, but their ideas about the underlying causes of black poverty were not very different. A close reading of the Moynihan Report does confirm that he repeatedly asserted that the problems he identified were not racial but rather were the product of mistreatment and discrimination. However, in the aftermath of the controversy Moynihan redoubled his emphasis on issues of pathology, and his politics and scholarship became increasingly ambivalent. O'Connor states: "It would be a mistake, then, to regard the Moynihan Report as principally a matter of liberal strategy gone awry. . . . Moynihan was . . . synthesizing themes that, if anything, would grow more pronounced in his work, and especially the theme that pathology, especially the dreaded welfare dependency, was a consequence of the absence of males from their rightful place as heads of families."[24]

Moynihan served as a domestic policy advisor to President Nixon and was author of the notion of "benign neglect" on issues of race, counseling the president to keep a low profile.[25] O'Connor credits him with supporting Nixon's efforts at eliminating welfare "dependency," and he was also associated with policies designed to get tough on inner city crime. He left the Nixon White House at the end of 1970 and returned to Harvard, where earlier he had joined the faculty in 1966 with the aid of James Q. Wilson, a conservative criminologist and later inventor of the controversial policy called "broken windows" policing.[26] In 1973, Nixon appointed Moynihan as US ambassador to India, and in 1975, President Ford appointed him as permanent representative to the United Nations. The following year he ran for the US Senate in New York and in the primary narrowly defeated Bella Abzug, a progressive feminist candidate. Moynihan won the general election and remained in the Senate for three additional terms, retiring in 2001. As senator, he reinstated his reputation as a liberal. He strongly opposed Reagan's assault on welfare spending and his expansion of the punitive programs Moynihan indirectly had helped install under Nixon. He was similarly opposed to the Personal Responsibility and Work Opportunity Act—the law President Clinton signed in 1996 that really did "end welfare as we knew it." Nevertheless, Clinton awarded him the Medal of Freedom in 2000, shortly before Hillary Clinton declared her ultimately successful candidacy to take over Moynihan's Senate seat. He died in 2003 at the age of seventy-six.

The Peculiar Strength of a Bad Idea

Moynihan is dead and virtually no one still reads the report he wrote back in 1965. Nonetheless, the ideas he popularized in his report are still very much alive, and his ownership of them is restated with remarkable frequency. George Will, conservative commentator, resurrected his image in August 2013 on the occasion of the fiftieth anniversary of the Civil Rights march on Washington: "A young social scientist from Harvard working in the Labor Department published a report. His name was Daniel Patrick Moynihan. He said, 'There is a crisis in the African-American community, because 24 percent of African-American children are born to unmarried women.' Today it's tripled to 72 percent. That, and not an absence of rights, is surely the biggest impediment [to black progress]." (George Will TV interview, *This Week with George Stephanopoulos*, August 25, 2013)

And yet more recently others have reprised Moynihan's connection to these ideas:

> Although conservatives look to family failings as an explanation for societal ills, this whole line of reasoning was also promoted by a liberal, Senator Daniel Patrick Moynihan. Moynihan attributed high crime rates to the rise of single parenthood in an influential 1986 report.[27] (Nigel Barber, *Huffington Post Parents*, February 6, 2014)

> Two major predictors of financial success/sustainability in America are, 1) Being born into existing poverty, and 2) Being raised in a one-parent home. If these factors are present when conceiving children, the statistical probability of successive generational poverty (one generation of the impoverished begetting another, ad infinitum) increases substantially. We have been acutely aware of this "phenomenon" since the 1960s, when Daniel Patrick Moynihan published his controversial report on the decline of the black nuclear family. (Chris Jepson, *Maitland/Winter Park Observer*, February 5, 2014)

These last two entries were pulled from a fairly long list of stories about Moynihan that resulted from my Google news search of mentions of him in the two days prior to the time of this writing, a more or less random outcropping of his contemporary fame. The ideas contained in the moldy report he hastily created in 1965 are very fresh indeed.[28]

William Ryan, Carol Stack, Herbert Gutman, James Farmer, and a legion of other effective critics notwithstanding, Moynihan's belief that family problems are at the heart of African American suffering continues to thrive. It was not a new idea when he put it forth, and his case was quite weak by conventional standards of sound scholarship. The reason it has survived as an iconic symbol is that he was a self-declared liberal intellectual, and his ideas came into public view at a moment when social politics were undergoing a fast pivot to the right. The report made him famous, and his fame has given life to the report long after the ashes of Watts have grown cold.

This book is about the idea, not the man or the adequacy of his report. Like George Will and the other commentators listed above, I am using Moynihan's report as a trope, a convenient device for exploring an abstraction that has plagued our society for far too long. Poverty begets two explanations: either the unfairness of the system causes many otherwise competent people to fail, or poor people are a collection of individuals who are simply deficient competitors in an otherwise fair economy. If the latter is correct, then smart and motivated offspring of poor families should have a better chance to succeed in life than stupid and lazy children of the rich. This deduction is manifestly untrue. Although some poor children do find their way to success and some rich kids come to naught, the actual proportions of these outcomes are very clearly quite small. Simple causes are rare in a complex universe, but logic and evidence favor the explanation that structural inequalities are the predominant reason we have so much poverty in our social system. So why is the other explanation so tenaciously attractive? What are the implications of this ungenerous and apparently illogical choice about how to think about social inequality?

The Moynihan Report and its undeserved influence do not explain why poor families, and not rigged opportunities, are blamed for huge inequalities of wealth and income. It is a tired old concept that some groups in society do not know how to raise children, and therefore they never get ahead, generation after generation. That some groups are naturally more successful than others is basically a conservative idea, deriving to some extent from Calvinist views of how God reveals his grace. Success is a badge of anointment. Hard work pays off, partly because it just does, and because God is watching and guiding those who please him. Poverty indicates the opposite, a sign of disfavor even when it is not accompanied by dissolute habits and apparent lassitude. There always has been an implicit distinction between the deserving and undeserving poor, but the line is very murky and in recent years precious little help has been available even for those considered to be deserving.[29]

In an earlier era, racism was a commonly accepted device for explaining social differences. Black people, especially, were considered to be inherently inferior and naturally prone to failure. Depending on the historical moment, such judgments were also heaped on the Irish, Slavs, Italians, Jews, Roma, Mexicans, Native Americans, Asians, and immigrants from anywhere that begets dark skin. To some extent, and varying by place and circumstance, these ideas are still embraced. But they are no longer socially acceptable.

Right-wing pundits can cover racism with explanations based on culture. The belief that bad parents raise children who cannot learn or control their impulses, develop bad values about work and family, and are attracted to substance abuse and crime—the essence of the tangle of pathology—offers an acceptable alternative mode of expressing prejudices against other groups, especially when such judgments appear to be free of ideology. When Pat Moynihan, liberal soldier in the War on Poverty, delivered this message, it was just what they were looking for, and it still works that way.

Liberals and ordinary apolitical citizens also have reasons to find this concept attractive. For many liberals, it suggests that change can be accomplished by rehabilitating the disadvantaged instead of carrying out the much harder task of challenging powerful forces responsible for the problem. "Blaming the victim" offers a seemingly tractable approach, and presumably grateful targets, for achieving social improvement. For the nonpoor, the vast majority of regular people who don't have to think too deeply about these matters, the idea that poverty is caused by inadequate parenting gives comfort in distinction and suggests that they have control over their lives. All they have to do to avoid being poor is to behave lawfully and raise their children right. They should not have to worry about becoming poor; they are essentially different and thus relatively safe.

Of course, the nonpoor are not really immune to misfortunes that can cause them to slip into poverty, as the aftermath of the mortgage meltdown of 2008 so amply revealed. In 2008 and 2009 I was involved in a research project on mortgage foreclosures that included interviews with many middle-class families who were in the process of losing their homes. Almost without exception, they blamed themselves and expressed intense shame that they had failed their families, that they had not had the protection they believed their class position and upbringing should have provided. However, rather than blame the scoundrels who sold them bad mortgages or the greedy bankers and traders who engineered this disaster, they too readily embraced the idea that they were losers. They had made bad choices and failed to exercise "personal responsibility."

The politics behind the idea that personal shortcomings are the cause of poverty and misfortune are very powerful. It is ironic, but unsurprising, that recessions tend to nurture increased emphasis on personal responsibility and deflection of blame that actually belongs elsewhere. In the early 1980s a recession lasted almost two years and caused the poverty rate to spike from around 12 percent to over 15 percent. It was also a period of rising support for very conservative political ideas. Ronald Reagan had been elected in a landslide over a sitting Democratic president (Jimmy Carter). During that period Charles Murray wrote a book titled *Losing Ground*[30] that articulated in very naked terms the idea that the social safety net reinforced bad behavior by poor people, and that the culture of the poor and the wrongheaded ideas of liberals were jointly responsible for the poverty that had grown so rapidly (not the recent recession and dramatic cutbacks in social spending). The vast popularity of this book inspired the liberal sociologist William Julius Wilson to take up the mantle that had been wrested from Moynihan almost two decades earlier by what Wilson described as fearful misguided social scientists and angry civil rights radicals. Wilson also published a very popular book, *The Truly Disadvantaged*,[31] in which he resurrected a liberal argument about family failure as an explanation for inner-city poverty, a condition that had grown tremendously under the policies of the Reagan administration (a coincidence he scarcely mentioned). Wilson's model did place substantial blame on the structural dislocations of suburbanization and deindustrialization, but he emphasized more strongly the role of broken families, defective values, and undisciplined social norms of inner-city residents in perpetuating the misery brought on by these larger societal shifts. He paid tribute to Moynihan and excoriated his liberal colleagues for being afraid to do likewise. Wilson claimed that the rapid and extremely negative response to the Moynihan Report had discouraged scholars in the ensuing period from risking similar wrath by simply avoiding cultural factors when discussing poverty. In so doing, he claimed, they had ceded that ground to Murray and other similarly conservative scholars.

Wilson's solution to this dilemma involved merging structural and cultural explanations. Like Moynihan, he placed original blame on the lack of adequate employment opportunities. Also like Moynihan, he focused attention on the sociocultural outcome of broken families and what he described as weak social control in neighborhoods of concentrated poverty. Wilson's influence on this discussion was very strong. He won awards, accolades, honorary degrees, and a distinguished professorship at Harvard. He undertook an ambitious and extensive research project on urban poverty and race and came to be regarded as the nation's leading expert on this subject. Partly in response to issues he raised, the Rockefeller Foundation and the Social Science Research Council undertook a massive project in the late 1980s to research this problem and come up with policy recommendations. Although the specific results of the project were disappointing, the urban and poverty policies that were crafted during the George H. W. Bush and Clinton administrations were heavily influenced by the thinking and research of leading participants in this effort.[32] Family values, personal responsibility, the economic importance of marriage, the need to encourage work, and the diminution of the role of the welfare state, were prominent features of policy making and research. Alongside these more conservative social policies was a rise in punitive laws about minor crime and drug use and a vast expansion of incarceration that most affected poor people of color.

With the turn of the twenty-first century, and the election of George W. Bush, these trends accelerated. Although Moynihan the senator had denounced this rightward turn, after his death he was lionized and memorialized for his earlier contributions to these same policies. As previous citations from the current decade indicate, he was praised for his foresight and credited with drawing attention to the growing problem of nonmarital child rearing and female-headed households. In 2009 the prestigious *Annals of the American Academy of Social and Political Science* published a special issue titled "The Moynihan Report Revisited," in which eminent social and political scientists praised his memory and his accomplishments. In 2013 the Urban Institute, the venerable center for liberal urban policy research, published a special report, also called "The Moynihan Report Revisited," which offered a similarly celebratory treatment of his legacy.

The Obama administration commenced in the grips of the most calamitous economic emergency since the Great Depression of the 1930s. The poverty rate again spiked to above 15 percent and has remained that high in spite of improvements in the rate of unemployment and a healthy recovery in the stock market. Social policies of the previous era have been largely continued, but the debate has begun to turn. These programs are not working. Poverty remains a stubborn problem that seems directly connected to disturbing levels of income inequality that are starting to surpass those of the late 1920s and resemble the gap of the early twentieth century, also known as the Gilded Age. That era gave birth to muckraking journalism, robust union activism, trust busting, and a settlement house movement that, although patronizing to a large degree, represented a serious attempt to ameliorate the dreadful poverty in which industrial workers of that period were mired.

It was, however, the nadir of race relations in this country, a time when lynching was common and Jim Crow segregation was spreading to virtually every sector of life in the South. Legal segregation has now ended, although many activists echo Michelle Alexander's slogan that mass incarceration is the "New Jim Crow."[33] Organized labor is at its lowest point in a century, and real wages have continued to decline for the vast majority of unskilled workers. Entrenched beliefs in the debasement of the poor and cultural deficiencies of African Americans and other ethnic minorities have remained a prominent feature of conservative ideology; and conservative beliefs about poverty are not radically different from those of many self-described liberal politicians and commentators. Both sides of the political spectrum continue to lament the rising rate of female-headed households, a condition now shared with white families in growing numbers. The tangle of pathology meme remains strong, a convenient idea that justifies punitive measures and stingy indifference to the needs of poor families and children. This book challenges that belief and attempts to disclose both its recent intellectual origins and the ways in which more productive and humane policies could be crafted to address the enormous problems facing our society today.

The following chapters are divided into two parts. Chapters 2 and 3 deal with issues related to research and theories about poverty and families, especially African American families. These chapters are designed to address the evidence and interpretations that lie at the heart of Moynihan's tangle of pathology thesis. This is not a replay of past controversies, or a condemnation of Moynihan for his shortcomings as a scholar and policy analyst, but rather an effort to lay out the theoretical and methodological issues behind contemporary thought on poverty and family structure. Chapters 4, 5, and

6 address contemporary policy issues that are directly affected by the culture of poverty/tangle of pathology mindset—the demonization and destruction of public housing; the criminalization of black youth and exoneration of wealthy financial criminals; and the profitable business of humiliating poor people by advising teachers, nonprofits, and social service personnel about the culture of poverty. The concluding chapter summarizes and synthesizes the main themes of the preceding chapters and offers alternative perspectives on ways to address constructively the problems that plague poor people in their daily lives.

2

Research and Politics

• • • • • • • • • • • • • • • • • •

The Culture of
Poverty Knowledge

> Today the sociologists are up to their necks in
> politics and have access to millions of govern-
> ment dollars, which, I am afraid, have been
> secured at the cost of propagating an image of
> the Negro condition which is apt to destroy
> our human conception of ourselves just at the
> moment when we are becoming politically free.
> —Ralph Ellison, interview in *Harper's*,
> March 1967

The quest for understanding about poverty and poor people, inquiries
predominantly conducted by those who are not poor themselves, is heavily freighted with the politics of knowledge and the myopia of race and
class. Here I will interrogate the varied process whereby Moynihan, his
detractors, and his supporters have pieced together and interpreted evidence about what causes poverty. Social distance between investigator and

the object of investigation poses an impediment in the discovery process, especially where class bias and ethnic differences intrude. There is tension between quantitative inference and qualitative understanding, and a hierarchy in the evidence that mirrors the social distance between intimate ethnography and a detached reading of sophisticated numerical data. Ethnographic researchers, who are the closest to people they are studying, typically reach very different conclusions about this problem and its causes than those who work at a distance and rely on statistical manipulation of large data sets.

In addition, significant political issues are at play in how data about poverty are interpreted. Research determining that poor people need and deserve higher levels of funding puts them in competition for scarce budgetary resources. Poor people have few lobbyists working on their behalf regardless of the strength of evidence. Such findings also beg the question of who is to blame for the distress of poor families. To what extent are societal racism and corporate greed responsible for the maldistribution of wealth and necessities? Who should pay to fix this problem? What might be the most successful approach? How does the production of knowledge interact with the contingencies of policy making in this highly controversial area of social investigation? This chapter cannot answer all of those questions, but their interconnectedness frames the discussion. Research on this topic is not simply a matter of empirical facts, but rather consists of myriad social and political layers that combine to determine public opinion and programs.

Culture and Poverty

Shortly before Moynihan launched the research for his report, a social science controversy erupted over whether poor people have a distinctive culture, i.e., a belief system and design for living that encourages irresponsible behavior and propagates failure from one generation to the next. Oscar Lewis, a well-known anthropologist, had published ethnographic research that purported to make that case. He labeled it the "culture of poverty," a catchy phrase that gained wide circulation and is still in common usage. Lewis had studied at Columbia University under some of the early titans of anthropology. Ruth Benedict was his PhD advisor, and Franz Boas also had some influence on his work. Benedict was famous for the book she wrote on Japanese culture during World War II for the War Department (*The Chrysanthemum and the Sword*, 1948). Her interpretations, made without benefit of fieldwork or solid data, drew very controversial conclusions about Japanese character development. Boas, considered by many to have been the father of American anthropology, was best known for his work on race. An exquisitely well-trained scientist, he drew on physical anthropology as well as ethnology to shatter ideas about race and biology, proving that no essential differences exist among so-called racial groupings.[1]

Geneticists later confirmed Boas's claims, demonstrating that race is a social construct, not a biological category. Boas's work, and the horrors of the Nazi regime, contributed to the scientific defeat of biological racism in the 1950s and beyond, but scarcely eliminated societal racism. At that time anthropologists conceived of culture as a kind of unitary variable that stamped individual group members with a common set of values and customs. Culture thus offered a subtle replacement for race as a term that could describe the same thing. The argument over ethnic differences ceased to be about biological heredity, becoming instead a difference about cultural inheritance. Benedict's work, under the mantle of "culture and personality" studies, contributed to this conceptual replacement of culture for biology. Another thread woven through the anthropology of that period was functionalism, the idea that cultural traits and practices are adaptive (i.e., fitness-enhancing) and intricately woven into the larger ecosystems supporting human groups. The human environment was both physical and social, evolving and changing but productive of mostly stable adaptations reflected in shared culture.

Out of this intellectual context, and his working-class family background, Oscar Lewis emerged as a very complex scholar. Generally identified as a Marxist, and undeniably sympathetic to the plight of the peasants and urban poor he studied, his work generated a tremendous amount of paradoxical attention because he apparently confirmed that poor people's behavior and values are chiefly responsible for their lack of success. "As an anthropologist I have tried to understand poverty and its associated traits as a culture . . . with its own structure and rationale, as a way of life which is passed down from generation to generation along family lines."[2] He based his theory on fieldwork with urban migrants in Puerto Rico and Mexico, enumerating a list of cultural traits that he believed were common to these and most poor communities in capitalist industrial societies. He argued that poor people are very oriented to the present, do not plan or delay gratification, are impulsive and prone to violence, are oversexed, are possessed of little ambition, and had a lot of other basically unflattering characteristics (about seventy distinct traits). Some in his list of traits are actually objective conditions of poverty, like unemployment, bad housing, and scarce food supplies. Lewis's main interest was family studies, granular ethnographies depicting relations among family members and the transmission of values and models of behavior. His writing was very lurid, filled with sex and conflict, and he achieved a wide popular audience unusual for anthropologists. Lewis also attracted a lot of criticism from other anthropologists, especially leftists involved with the Civil Rights movement, and Mexican and Puerto Rican nationalists who reacted against demeaning ethnic portraits in his work.[3] The government of Mexico unsuccessfully sued him for publishing pornography and suggesting that Mexicans were sexually depraved.[4] Similar to Moynihan, Lewis was accused of "blaming the victim" and deflecting attention away from structural inequities and onto the dysfunctional behavior of individuals and families.

The backlash against Lewis's thesis in anthropology occurred within the same time frame as the initially negative response to Moynihan. Lewis's first major publication on this topic, *Five Families: Mexican Case Studies in the Culture of Poverty*, came out in 1959, followed by a spate of articles in the early '60s and his book about Puerto Ricans (*La Vida*) in 1965.[5] Lewis knew Moynihan personally, and they directly exchanged ideas and written work. Carol Stack, who was a graduate student at the University of Illinois in 1966 and just beginning work on what would be one of the most effective challenges to both men's ideas, tells of a breakfast meeting to which she was invited where Moynihan handed a copy of his report to Lewis and the two engaged in animated but agreeable conversation about their shared ideas. Moynihan reportedly said, "I love your culture of poverty concept."[6]

According to Barbara Ehrenreich, Michael Harrington, author of another highly influential book on poverty written in this same period (*The Other America*, 1962), also loved Lewis's idea. Speaking about Harrington, she wrote: "According to him, what distinguished the poor was their unique 'culture of poverty,' a concept he borrowed from Oscar Lewis, who had derived it from his study of Mexican slum-dwellers. That concept gave *The Other America* a trendy academic twist, but it also gave the book a conflicted double message."[7] Somewhat later in the same article, Ehrenreich describes Harrington as one of Moynihan's "drinking companions at the famed White Horse Tavern in Greenwich Village." So, the trio of purveyors of this controversial and contradictory idea, liberals of various stripes sympathetic to the downtrodden and hoping to influence public practices and policy, are known to have broken bread and imbibed with each other in pursuit of comity and shared understanding.[8]

It is unclear how much they may have influenced each other's beliefs about cultural practices and the persistence of poverty. The details of their relationships are much less important than the impact of their work and the politics and substance of the responses they drew. An important dimension to all of their arguments was the acknowledgment that exploitation and racism were primary factors shaping the cultural differences they observed. Harrington was especially consistent on this point, and his use of the term *culture of poverty* has a meaning different from either Lewis's or Moynihan's. In *The Other America*, Harrington makes no mention of Lewis, although he cites many other social scientists and economists. He does make ubiquitous mention of the "culture of poverty," but he seems to have lifted the phrase without buying the whole concept.[9] Maurice Isserman, writing in 2012 (the fiftieth anniversary of the book's 1962 publication), offers the following:

> Harrington's success . . . would have ironic consequences. *The Other America*
> popularized the phrase "culture of poverty," which went on to shape the main
> thrust of Johnson's war on poverty. But a close reading of Harrington's book
> reveals an ambiguity in his employment of that term. Throughout the book
> he used "culture of poverty" interchangeably with another term, "vicious
> circle." . . . But nothing in the "vicious circle" he sketched above was culturally
> determined in the sense that Oscar Lewis had meant when he talked of . . .
> an ingrained and unchanging way of life passed down from generation to
> generation.

Isserman, clearly an admirer of Harrington, goes on to say that the implication of this different use of the term was that Harrington believed this problem could be "improved through the simple expedient of additional household income."[10] Moynihan and Lewis also believed that the transmission of poverty culture could be altered, but their remedies were more extreme and unlikely. Moynihan wanted the government to intervene in shaping a more conventional kinship system for African Americans, and Lewis wanted poor people to engage in a revolution against the state.

The use of melodramatic language and descriptions also linked these three contemporaneous writers about poverty. Their biographers speculate that this stylistic approach was intended to attract attention and sympathy among the general public. These extremities were supposed to inspire action and bring forth demands for assistance. The main consumers of their ideas about poverty, however, were conservatives who wanted the state to do nothing to help these depraved poor people, and moderate liberals who espoused therapeutic approaches for rescuing salvageable individuals ensnared in a vicious culture. The complexity of the personal politics and underlying motives of Lewis, Moynihan, and Harrington were lost in the reductionism of their sensational appeals. The excitement generated by salacious prose obscured the nuance of their liberal interpretations. Grasping this paradox is critical to understanding how well-meaning leftists could have spawned such a venomous industry of condemnation.

Bashing Oscar and Pat

Lewis and Moynihan had many admirers, but they also faced a barrage of criticism over the implications of their work. Their defenders complained that critics were ignoring the virtues and sensibilities of these two men, and that their work was being misunderstood and misrepresented. Another thread in the rebuke against the critics, one that emerged in later years, was that allegedly thuggish treatment of Moynihan and Lewis by their academic opponents and political enemies had intimidated more reasonable liberal researchers from seriously examining the cultural causes of poverty for fear of suffering a similar fate. This cowardly aversion allegedly opened a void in the larger inquiry that allowed ultraconservatives to ply the cultural argument as a simple-minded excuse for cutting social programs. More will be said of this later. In defense of the critics, the focus of their attention had more to do with the negative impact of these concepts—"tangle of pathology" and "culture of poverty"—than with presumptive motives of the authors of these ideas. Moreover, the critics in many cases offered substantive criticism of methods, data, and interpretation, not ideological complaints about the unfortunate implications of otherwise sound findings. Shortcomings in research design, data analysis, and interpretive logic were fair targets for criticism, especially of a document that was attracting a high level of policy interest.

Lewis and Moynihan employed very different methods. Lewis was almost purely qualitative, offering long passages of straight transcriptions from interviews and field notes with little interpretation, summed up at the end with his theory about culture and poverty. Moynihan's report, on the other hand, relied heavily on quantitative data, although without much analysis. He also used secondary sources about African American families and culture, doing no primary research of his own on that topic.

Lewis's treatment of the culture concept was deliberately fashioned out of anthropological logic and analysis. He viewed poor people as having a distinct "subculture."[11] Their way of life was described as an adaptation to the circumstances of economic insufficiency. Deviant behavior, such as prostitution, was a reaction to the need for income in the absence of reputable opportunities. Although functionally determined, behaviors and attitudes that developed were unacceptable to the larger society, and when transmitted to children resulted in intergenerational disadvantage. Reflecting the culture and personality school, he believed that children as young as six became indelibly imprinted with the value system learned within their families. Here were the alleged mechanisms that transformed the desperation of poverty into a self-perpetuating cultural trap. This idea was quite similar to Moynihan's assertion that the tangle of pathology was passed on to children, who learned bad habits from their mothers and the void left by absent fathers. It is not hard to see why they found agreement, and how Lewis could have influenced Moynihan's ideas. Although anthropology was evidently useful in this regard, Moynihan did not similarly utilize the extensive literature on kinship that would have called into question his conviction that patriarchal nuclear families were some kind of universal norm. I will address that issue in the next chapter.

The most effective critics of Lewis's work were other anthropologists. Eleanor Leacock, who also studied at Columbia a decade after Lewis, organized a special symposium at the 1966 meetings of the American Anthropological Association to discuss the culture of poverty concept and Oscar Lewis's use of this term. From that meeting came an edited volume entitled *The Culture of Poverty: A Critique*.[12] Most of the contributors were anthropologists, but a few psychologists, educators, and sociologists were among the authors of the fourteen articles, most of which strongly disputed Lewis's ideas about poverty and culture. Leacock's introduction compares and equates Lewis and Moynihan, and concludes that both have distorted the meaning of culture and facts about the groups who are described. "Not only does the poverty-culture theory focus on a negative, distorted and truncated view of a cultural whole, but it also implies an untenable view of the process whereby cultural traits are evolved and transmitted."[13]

Leacock contended that humans are more plastic than Lewis suggested, that they are not determined by their earliest experiences but rather can learn and change throughout childhood and beyond. Based on her own research in low-income schools, she also argued that the negative reinforcement children receive from teachers and other authority figures, where they are deliberately prepared for low-skill and low-status positions in life, has a greater impact on their destinies than their family experiences. Finally, she claimed that the judgmental language Lewis used in interpreting the traits he enumerated is "ethnocentric," based on implicit assumptions about the superiority of middle-class values. In addition to criticizing his interpretive framework, she also focused on the effect this work had on existing bigotry and stereotypes that condemn people who are poor, especially those who are also black or brown. She speculated that this portrayal reinforces feelings of superiority on the part of working-class Americans who "argue that it takes will and ability to get ahead, and that the poor are poor out of laziness, stupidity, or lack of ambition. He [the nonpoor person] thereby not only vindicates his own gains, and assuages, perhaps, a lingering guilt that he does not wish to cast behind a helping hand, but he also reassures himself. It is important to him that his position should follow from an intrinsically greater worthiness; this helps protect him from the threat of social vagaries like the rise and fall of unemployment."[14]

Another ardent critic of Lewis was Charles Valentine, an anthropologist who was doing an extended ethnographic study in Harlem with his African American wife, Bettylou, who also was an anthropologist. Valentine published a chapter in Leacock's book and also wrote his own book, *Culture and Poverty* (1968).[15] Like Leacock, he contended that Lewis had "abused" the concept of culture and the value of ethnography. Valentine extracted numerous examples from the narratives of Lewis's subjects that contradict the basic tenets of the theory. The limited number of individuals included in *La Vida* and the unrepresentative nature of their lives was the basis for another criticism. He claimed that an ethnography should have sufficient scope to encompass the variations within groups that are studied. Lewis's study did not, but rather had constructed provocative and disturbing portraits of a few families who were deliberately selected for their deviance. Finally, Valentine noted that Lewis failed to analyze fully the ways external pressures and structures that oppress families like the ones he studied are a critical part of the larger culture, and go a long way to explain their responses. More generally, Valentine argued that ethnographies of communities within complex societies should be contextualized. Qualitative accounts have the virtue of capturing critical details and human understanding that statistics cannot convey. However, the fact that they cannot be falsified provides great latitude to the ethnographer's editing and interpretation. Valentine and other critics claimed that Lewis's poetic license produced an exaggerated narrative and unwittingly destructive use of anthropological methods.

Other anthropologists of that period and somewhat later provided portraits of poor people in the inner cities of the US that differed importantly, both in texture and interpretation, from those in Lewis's work. Elliot Liebow published a landmark ethnography of "streetcorner men" in Washington, DC in 1967 (*Tally's Corner*).[16] It was done within a larger study conducted by the African American sociologist, Hylan Lewis, "Child Rearing Practices among Low Income Families in the District of Columbia," carried out in 1962–1963 (and not referenced in the Moynihan Report). Hylan Lewis was a pointed critic of the Moynihan Report and a contributor to Leacock's critical volume about the culture of poverty. Liebow, a white anthropologist, conducted an extended ethnographic field study on a single corner in the inner-city slums of Washington, DC. His focus was on a relatively small group of men who gathered there on a regular basis and had very unstable or no employment. They were the epitome of failure—in life, marriage, and parenting.

Liebow's interpretation of these very poor and frequently depressed men, perfect examples of a culture of poverty, rejected that characterization. Rather than exhibiting deviant adaptive strategies that renounced the importance of middle-class ideals, they were tortured by their inability to achieve that status, although artful in fashioning relationships with each other that allowed themselves a measure of dignity and satisfaction. Rather than a tangle of pathology, Liebow saw a struggle for normalcy and a very clear indication that the defining problem they faced was the absence of opportunities to have decent work and economically stable lives. The study was conducted in the same city where Moynihan was writing his report for the US Department of Labor; it was sponsored by a federal grant. Moynihan apparently knew nothing about it, although when Liebow's book came out, two years after his report, Moynihan wrote in a blurb for the cover that *Tally's Corner* was "nothing short of brilliant—a work of importance."

A very similar study, also taking place in Washington, DC at the same time as Liebow's, was done by a Swedish anthropologist, Ulf Hannerz, author of *Soulside*, published in 1969.[17] As a doctoral student, he studied an inner-city block he called "Winston Street." Like Liebow, his focus was narrow and deep. He hung around, explained himself somehow, and gained the acquaintance of a large number of the local inhabitants. His account is similar to Liebow's. The sad facts of lives he describes do not differ greatly from what Moynihan details in his litany of pathology. He confirms the instability of marriage, but shows how instrumental and external are the impediments to stability. He also gives a fully rounded portrayal of residual warmth and creativity not smothered by struggle. The anguish of failure, and the resourcefulness of many who are struggling for dignity and peace, links the people of Winston Street to the rest of humankind and disputes the idea of a cultural trap. It is not their culture that is weighing them down, but a life of scarcity and injustice. These miseries are both embellished and mitigated by qualities Hannerz describes as "soul," the deeply felt and sometimes celebrated spirituality and irrepressible search for creative meaning in life.

All Our Kin, by Carol Stack, provided the most widely cited ethnographic case against the culture of poverty, and especially Moynihan's family values lament.[18] Set in a fictionalized Illinois city neighborhood called "The Flats," Stack describes everyday life among poor black people. She took her young son with her into the neighborhood and made friends with other mothers. Her approach was very personable, and her presence was tolerably welcomed. From her close observations of how life was lived and what strategies could be detected, she wrote a story mainly from the viewpoint of women, and sketched out a ramified kinship system that promoted mutual aid and was far more efficacious than Moynihan's rendering. More will be said about this contrast in the next chapter, but as ethnography, Stack's work provided intimate images and tangible texture, an insider account like those of Liebow and Hannerz. Kinship was not an obstruction, but rather offered channels along which poverty could be managed more collectively. The external pressures identified by Liebow and Hannerz are ever present in the Flats and are no less damaging than in the other accounts. All three ethnographies share a nuanced interpretation of "ghetto" culture that reveals the human impacts of, and responses to, economic and social inequality.

Quantitative Arguments

Valentine's critique of Moynihan centered on his use of quantitative data, and his association with Nathan Glazer and the work of E. F. Frazier, a well-known African American sociologist (who had died not long before the controversies analyzed here broke out). Valentine described Frazier's work as a "pejorative tradition of class culture . . . forcefully extended by such contemporary scholars as Nathan Glazer and Daniel Patrick Moynihan . . . in the recent book, *Beyond the Melting Pot*," a comparative study of ethnicity in New York City (described at length in chapter 1).[19] Valentine condemned Glazer's assertions about African American "broken homes and illegitimacy" as based solely on census and other statistical data, which suffered from varied sources of unreliability. He then expended several pages in critique of Moynihan's report, which he dismissed as "very little more than another updated rehash of Frazier," and he traced the methods and message to the book that Moynihan coauthored with Glazer.[20] Once again, his principal argument was with Moynihan's exclusive reliance on census data and other official statistics in formulating broad inferences about matrifocality and the emasculation of black men, leading to a speculative host of other failures and vices that are similarly adduced from statistical data of questionable reliability. He contended that such data offered a misleading and incomplete picture of life in poor black neighborhoods, like Harlem where Valentine and his family had learned rich lessons from their ethnographic research. Valentine concluded his critique of Moynihan with a complaint that he blamed the problems facing poor black people on the "internal deficiencies of their own way of life," rather than the discrimination that kept them in poverty.[21] Finally, he decried the fact that no proposal for action was included in the report, just a diagnosis reinforcing existing prejudiced ideas about black culture.

Herbert Gans, a sociologist who had done an ethnographic study of Boston's West End, *The Urban Villagers* (1962), offered a similar critique of Moynihan's failure to make programmatic or even policy recommendations. Gans's criticism is very gentle, especially compared with Valentine's and those in selections in Leacock's book. Gans wrote soon after the report was released, in October 1965. In understated criticism he makes the same case as the others: "Of course, the deterioration of Negro society is due both to lack of opportunity and to cultural deprivation, but the latter is clearly an effect of the former, and is much more difficult to change through government policies."[22] He worried that emphasizing the cultural explanation could lead to "pseudo-psychiatric programs that attempt to change the Negro family through counseling and other therapeutic methods" (a concern that later materialized during the administrations of Bush II and Obama, under the label of "marriage promotion"). Gans proceeded to offer his own ideas about what kinds of programs might address the true causes of black poverty—public works jobs, a higher minimum wage, changes in the rules of welfare to support two-parent families, low-income housing outside of the ghetto, better schools, etc. In implicit criticism of Moynihan's hasty methods, he recommends "a massive research program on the structure of the Negro family" to determine needs and whether assertions of pathology were in fact accurate. He argued that, with better empirical understanding, it could be determined whether families could be aided more effectively by simply insuring adequate income. He also suggested that kinship structures need not follow middle-class rules to provide adequate nurturing for children. Valentine's book contains a fairly lengthy section on Gans, which, among other praise, cites the meticulous documentation of his methods for doing ethnographic research among working-class Italians.

William Ryan, then a psychologist at the Harvard Medical School and an early critic of Moynihan, wrote a widely circulated article published in the *Nation* magazine in November 1965, shortly after the release of the report, that focused on the uncritical use of quantitative data that had been gathered for other purposes. Moynihan, he argued,

> draws dangerously inexact conclusions from weak and insufficient data; encourages (no doubt unintentionally) a new form of subtle racism that might be termed "Savage Discovery" [the title of his article], and seduces the reader into believing that it is not racism and discrimination but the weaknesses and defects of the Negro himself that account for the present status of inequality between Negro and white. The document can be criticized on three levels: first, the methodological weaknesses; second, the manifest misstatements; and finally, the naive error of interpreting statistical relationships in cause-and-effect terms.[23]

Ryan made a compelling case for unacknowledged problems with the data Moynihan used on rates of "illegitimacy." He claimed the official data were unreliable indicators of norms or behavior, based on the wider options of middle-class white girls who got pregnant during the same period. They could alter their embarrassing condition through adoption, abortion, or a coerced marriage. He also contended that poor black girls had little access to contraception, unlike their white middle-class counterparts, and were less able or willing to place an unplanned baby up for adoption. Finally, middle-class white births before or without marriage were much more likely not to appear in the official records as illegitimate. The thrust of his argument was that in focusing on illegitimacy, Moynihan drew a portrait of African American women as promiscuous, when actually there was little difference between black and white teenagers in the incidence of premarital sex.

Hylan Lewis, in a paper prepared in November 1965, also addressed fallacies in the Moynihan Report (without naming it) that echo some of Ryan's objections.[24] Lewis pointed out the importance of controlling for income when making black-white comparisons, something Moynihan failed to do. Lewis's critique was very methodical and supported with statistical data from government sources that would have been available to Moynihan. He argued that cause and effect had become twisted, that the correlations reported by Moynihan reflected the effects of poverty rather than its causes. This theme is pervasive in the general stream of criticisms of Moynihan's report. Criticism of his handling of statistics and challenges to the validity of his assumptions about history, culture, and gender were the core of the negative reactions to the report. A few were angry, even vituperative, but the vast majority of published rejoinders were courteous and concerned with the substance of findings and interpretations, not the motives or character of Moynihan and his team.

Laura Carper, a human rights activist and member of the Michigan Civil Rights Commission, labeled by detractors as a "feminist," offered a highly critical response to Moynihan in a Spring 1966 article in *Dissent* magazine.[25] She began with a quote from Sean O'Casey's play, *Juno and the Paycock*, where a deserted Irish mother declares good riddance to her faithless irresponsible spouse. She also drew similar examples from tales of family life in the Jewish *shetls* of rural Russia. Her point was that happy intact families are hard to sustain in all impoverished and despised ethnic groups. A more incisive criticism in her article, however, was her dissection of Moynihan's favorite statistical finding. He claimed to have irrefutable evidence that black poverty had become a self-perpetuating problem, unaffected by external changes in employment opportunities. This claim was based on an inverse correlation he discovered between the increased enrollment of black women on welfare during the same years (1962–1964) that unemployment among black men had declined. In other words, it appeared that illegitimacy and "dependency" were growing in spite of improved opportunities to form conventional families headed by working males. Moynihan seized on this counterintuitive result, saying it revealed "clear indications that the situation may indeed have begun to feed on itself."[26] The graph of these two variables that is printed on page 13 of the report shows an abrupt change of direction in 1963, when welfare enrollment spiked and nonwhite male unemployment dipped. This relationship created an X on the graph, an inverse trend, that has come to be known as "Moynihan's scissors."

Moynihan's Scissors

Carper, Ryan, and many other early critics claimed that Moynihan had confused cause and effect in the correlations he drew from the tables and charts included in the report. Moynihan himself conceded that it was difficult to determine if fragile marriages were the cause of poverty or simply an effect of the unstable employment of black men. But in his graph entitled "Cases Opened Under AFDC Compared with Unemployment Rate for Nonwhite Males," he claimed to have found inarguable evidence that the cultural affliction favoring matrifocal families had taken root so firmly that it was growing even as the presumed cause, men without jobs, was moving in the other direction. The women apparently had come to prefer the narcotic dependency of welfare payments over the respectable stability of marriage to a male provider. Moynihan presented this single correlation as definitive evidence of the contagious pathology he feared. He believed that "there will be no social peace in the United States for generations" unless these family problems could be solved. In the aftermath of the Watts rioting, his prediction about social unrest was quoted frequently in the press.

That there was a connection between employment and family stability was not questioned; the controversy was over the direction of influence. If more/better jobs equal greater stability, then policy should just be to make jobs. If, however, employment growth has ceased to promote the formation of traditional families, then family values become the focus of attention. Moynihan's unstated project was to demonstrate that the culture of poverty, exemplified by "crumbling" families, was the principal driver of black-white economic disparities. He argued that a single inverse correlation between jobs and welfare, over a three-year period, offered conclusive evidence in favor of this interpretation. This small finding emerged as the key to the argument—a cold hard number hinting at a wide panoply of cultural dysfunctions. Alice O'Connor emphasized Moynihan's belief that he "sealed the argument that the 'pathology' had become self-perpetuating: pathology, here measured as welfare 'dependency,' was no longer correlated with the unemployment rate; it was going up on its own." It was a frail reed upon which to balance such a controversial claim. O'Connor challenged the meaning of the finding and the validity of the measures, recapping the evidence against this interpretation. "The fact is that the statistical correlation 'proved' nothing of the sort. As studies at the time and subsequently indicated, unemployment and economic recession were never more than partial explanations for changes in welfare enrollment rates."[27]

Occurring at the same time the rates of enrollment had begun to rise (1962) were reforms to the welfare system that eased eligibility, enabling an expansion of benefits to those not previously reached. These changes, together with continued migration of African Americans from stingy southern states to northern cities where welfare was accessible, offer a more parsimonious explanation of the steep rise in enrollments. Laura Carper made the same point in 1966. She also pointed out that Moynihan's measure of nonwhite male unemployment rates was cast too broadly by including all age groups. The rates for young black males were substantially higher and rising, not falling, during the period measured. More than one in four (27 percent) young black men (18–19) was unemployed in 1963 (up from 24 percent in 1961), compared with the scissors rate of 10% for all black men (down from 13% in 1961).[28] Fathers of the babies whose mothers were signing up for welfare would likely be the young men who were still struggling to find work. Finally, she noted that Moynihan completely omitted female employment from his analysis, a critical variable in household budgets and decision making. During the period of the anomalous drop in overall nonwhite male unemployment, the rates for both young black men and women remained stubbornly high and consistent with increased welfare enrollment. O'Connor added another caveat about the unemployment data Moynihan relied on; men who were not participating in the labor force were not included in the measure. A very large number of young black men were not in the labor force for various reasons, almost none good; and they also were likely to be well represented among the fathers of the babies in question. Both Carper and O'Connor agree that the measures Moynihan used as the answer to this question were highly flawed. His cultural explanation for sharp increases in welfare enrollment competed poorly against coincidental regulatory changes that greatly expanded eligibility.

Carper's critique, which O'Connor substantially repeated in 2001, was published in April 1966, eight months after the release of the report. It was a very early, and well publicized, refutation of the critical finding that reportedly confirmed Moynihan's basic thesis of self-perpetuating pathology. Carper's evidence was empirical, and she identified multiple basic weaknesses in the argument Moynihan based on a scissors-like configuration on a single graph. As "science" the famous "Moynihan Scissors" does not meet standards of empirical evidence, and does not confirm the elaborate theoretical explanation he offered or justify the emphasis given it in the media. It was, and should have become known as, a weak, misleading, and flawed analysis. Instead, however, it has survived as the catchy nugget of scientific evidence that Moynihan was able to tease out of the mass of spurious correlations he had charted. The scissors name was invented by Moynihan's friend James Q. Wilson, a previously identified Harvard criminologist. There was scant to no effort on the part of Moynihan's supporters to defend or replicate his finding. Carper's critique was perhaps sufficient to demonstrate the folly that would come from efforts to vindicate this dubious claim.

However, politicians and journalists have continued to cite the scissors finding as conclusive proof that Moynihan was right. In the two weeks prior to this writing, George Will, conservative commentator, published a column in the *Washington Post* invoking the scissors as evidence that Republican plans to cut safety net programs are sound policy.[29] Through the years, there have been frequent references to the scissors finding in popular media. Moynihan himself cited this example long after Carper and others had discredited it. In a 1990 article in the magazine *Society*, Moynihan recounted the discovery of the scissors and mentioned James Q. Wilson's role in naming it. In this piece he generalized the scissors measure, which he insinuated was an indicator of indecency and irresponsibility, to the whole generation who came of age in the 1960s. He lamented, "I would prefer to have it called the 'sixties scissors.' But call it as you like, it really was a scissors." Not explaining what he meant by that, he proceeded to connect the inverse correlation in his original finding with other selected recent social correlations also showing divergent trends, as if an inverted correlation was itself a meaningful condition. He suggested ominously that "*Something* happened [emphasis in original]. Something which, if we did not quite understand, at least we spotted." Looking back over twenty-five years at social and cultural trends he viewed as negative, he pronounced his original discovery as not just correct, but capturing a woeful sea change in how society works. He specifically decried the expanding number of "illegitimate" births (the rate was then actually growing faster among white than black mothers, but both had risen sharply over the decades since 1965): "I put it to you that we forecast some of this but that nobody was listening. When I wrote what I did in 1965, the hypothesis was rejected. It was said, 'this is not so.' And then it turned out that it was so. I saw it coming in the data, and I said this is going to happen, and we are going to be unhappy about it."[30]

Long after the scissors measure had been refuted, Moynihan clung to its alleged significance. The real measure of his scholarship, he seemed to believe, lay in its prescience, not in its technical precision. He had warned that the family was the key to social well-being and that it was threatened by the declining importance of marriage. His unheeded warnings had come to pass, and he felt vindicated.

Revival

Influential social scientists in the 1980s reinforced that judgment, elevating Senator Moynihan into the pantheon of liberal intellectual heroes and rehabilitating the Moynihan Report. The impetus for this shift was complicated. Reagan's election in 1980 ushered in a new era of conservative politics and a repudiation of the War on Poverty. The war is over and poverty won, President Reagan had quipped. Slashing social programs and attacking unions was the action that followed. As mentioned earlier, Charles Murray, then a fellow at the conservative Manhattan Institute, published *Losing Ground* in 1984. In it he revived the most pejorative features of the culture of poverty argument in an assault on lower-class behavior and what he believed were misguided social programs. During that same period, William Julius Wilson was developing an impressive research program in Chicago on inner-city poverty, which had gotten much worse during the eighties. Wilson was offended and aroused by the attention Murray's work had drawn, but instead of blaming Reagan's harmful policies, he blamed the critics of Moynihan.

Wilson attributed Murray's popularity to a general longing for poverty explanations that included culture, reinstating aspects of the culture of poverty theory. A moderate view on deep poverty (the condition of the "underclass") was emerging that was less challenging over the need for systemic change, conciliatory on matters related to culture.[31] Wilson claimed that Moynihan had presented the problem as a combined result of culture and a limited opportunity structure, but his balanced message was drowned out by spiteful critics. Murray's reactionary version emphasizing culture was instead dominating the conversation. Missing were fair-minded liberal scholars who might have advanced Moynihan's idea. A scold developed to the effect that the bruising criticism leveled against Moynihan in 1965 and after—unfair leftist attacks motivated by ideology—had intimidated a whole generation of urban researchers from even entertaining ideas about culture and poverty. Everyone was afraid of being treated the same way as Pat, so they simply did not venture into that topical area. This reputed abstention left an empty space in the conversation that was gladly filled by conservatives, seeking to provide evidence that poor people were harmed by welfare and responsible for their own plight. Wilson claimed that Moynihan had been right about most of what he believed, and that the value of his work had been lost in the controversy.

Moynihan's correct prediction of worse poverty and greater family instability was deemed sufficient to vindicate him, and there certainly was ample basis for such a reassessment. Between 1965 and 1985, rates of divorce, unmarried parenting, and female-headed households had skyrocketed. The number of families in poverty also went way up. To that extent, Moynihan had been right. However, he still could have been wrong about the meaning and causes of these changes. Moynihan posited a self-perpetuating mechanism in the cultural values of poor black families. Wilson and his research assistant, Kathryn Neckerman, wrote an entire chapter in *The Truly Disadvantaged* on male unemployment, female-headed households, and poverty. They confirmed close linkages between employment and marriage, while implicitly disconfirming Moynihan's scissors thesis. Although Wilson and Neckerman do not state this connection in their chapter, O'Connor prominently included their analysis among the studies that repudiated the scissors, finding that "welfare and unemployment had not, as the Moynihan Report suggested, somehow become 'unglued.'"[32]

During the 1980s conditions in inner cities for poor black families markedly worsened. In 1983, a recession year, the overall poverty rate spiked to over 15 percent. The unemployment rate for African American youth 16–19 years old exceeded 50 percent and stayed very high for the next five years. Also rising was the rate of single-parent households and the proportion of children born to unmarried parents. Contrary to the scissors formula, welfare benefits declined by 10 percent in constant dollars between 1980 and 1985. In this time frame, welfare spending went down while black youth unemployment was rising—a mirror-image inverse correlation that drew no attention from Moynihan or Wilson. Just as the rise in welfare spending measured in 1963 reflected shifting policies, so did the decline in 1980s benefits reflect a political decision to cut that funding. In addition to shrinking benefits and job opportunities, inner-city neighborhoods became major hubs of street traffic in illegal drugs in the 1980s. Associated violence and rising rates of arrest and incarceration visited new afflictions on the residents of these places. Settings for 1980s research by Wilson, his colleagues, and students at the University of Chicago offered a full plate of misery. Chapters 4 and 5, on housing issues and incarceration, address these sites and studies more directly. For this chapter, however, the research directions these scholars charted during the 1980s are critical for understanding contemporary issues and the dominant epistemology behind poverty research.

Wilson has exerted enormous influence; he combined a prodigious research program with an analysis that fit well with neoliberal ideas about personal responsibility, individualism, and enlightened social engineering. There were three strands of urban poverty research during the period between the late 1980s and early 2000s: mainstream liberals and moderates, exemplified by Wilson and his collaborators; neoconservatives, represented by Charles Murray and others on the right; and left-leaning critics of neoliberal policies and research agendas.

The main left opposition has consisted of a loose group of anthropologists, geographers, and sociologists who have continued the critique of Moynihan (implicitly or directly), disputed the wisdom of his original contribution, and basically rejected the idea of a culture of poverty as shaped by Moynihan or Oscar Lewis. The larger system of global capital, politics, and the drive to privatize the public sector are viewed as the principal generators of poverty. Unemployment, displacement, crumbling schools, and declining public and social services result from elite-level decisions and projects, not from the cultural preferences of poor people. Perhaps the best-known urban critic has been David Harvey, a cultural geographer at CUNY Grad Center who has written extensively on neoliberal politics and policies, and on a crusade he labels the "right to the city." His writing centers on the rise of capitalist political power in the 1980s and the neoliberal policies that have transformed urban economies and brought forth growing inequality. Stephen Steinberg, a sociologist also at CUNY, has written extensively on the revanchism of the 1980s and the negative influence of culture of poverty thinking.[33] Carol Stack has continued to publish on the kinship of poor people and the resistance of the racist establishment to organized change.[34] The work of Robin Kelley, a cultural historian who has criticized mainstream characterizations of African American families, offers another example of this perspective.[35] Adolph Reed, professor of political science at the University of Pennsylvania, has also offered substantial critiques of neoliberalism in academia and politics.[36] There are many more, well beyond the scope of this discussion.

The drastic welfare legislation of 1996 (The Personal Responsibility and Work Opportunity Act) initiated much critical research, especially by anthropologists. Sandra Morgen and Jeff Maskovsky wrote a 2003 review of ethnographic research on welfare reform that challenges the findings and conclusions of quantitative, what they call "mainstream," poverty research.[37] Brett Williams's 2004 monograph, *Debt for Sale*, examined the link between poverty and growing indebtedness in a compelling study that presaged the mortgage and student debt crises.[38] A compendium of articles by these and other authors was published in 2001, edited by Judith Goode and Jeff Maskovsky, titled *The New Poverty Studies*.[39] The most comprehensive and influential work has been done by Alice O'Connor, historian and social critic, who wrote the book *Poverty Knowledge*, a century-long history of US policy and research, in 2001. She details the struggles in the Office of Economic Opportunity over community organizing versus therapeutic approaches to perceived cultural deficiencies. Her personal involvement in a well-funded effort during the 1980s by the Social Science Research Council and the Rockefeller Foundation to assemble scholars, researchers, policy experts, and practitioners in pursuit of a clear understanding of the problem and potential solutions, offers a revealing vantage on the political and academic tensions surrounding this issue.[40] In her analysis, the "mainstream" forces dominated the effort to the disadvantage of other views and diminished the capacity to reach a workable consensus.

The mainstream at that time consisted of Wilson and his colleagues at Chicago and other universities, and the national research establishment that had developed over the decades since the War on Poverty was launched, most prominently the Urban Institute and the Brookings Institution. The work of these scholars—mainly sociologists, political scientists, and economists—was highly quantitative and incorporated cultural as well as structural variables in modeling poverty's causes and consequences. Right-wing researchers like Murray, but also Lawrence Mead, Thomas Sowell, Dinesh D'Souza, and others, worked out of the Manhattan Institute, the American Enterprise Institute, and other nonprofit and academic think tanks that embraced very conservative views on poverty and poor people. Moynihan has been iconic for both the mainstream liberals and the neocons; his symbolic value resides in his political identity as a Kennedy Democrat, who was also a PhD urban expert and a respected liberal US senator. His early work has become hallowed by both sides, because his criticisms of the black community cannot be attributed to malice. Emphasizing culture in the study of poverty offered liberal researchers a bridge to a political establishment that was aggressively illiberal and actively rewriting the social contract. Revisioning the culture versus structure divide in theorizing poverty to include dual causation and feedback loops permitted conversation across ideological divides and enabled progress for research programs. Burnishing the image of Moynihan has been part of that conversation.

Herbert Gans, whose initial reply to the report had been measured and not specifically critical of design or execution, reread it in 2010, amidst a large amount of attention to Moynihan that will be described shortly. Gans revisited the report through the eyes of someone who had been there all along. He limited his criticisms to what Moynihan could have known and done in 1965. His account of this examination begins with a verdict: "Moynihan himself made significant contributions to antipoverty policy later in his career, but his Report does not deserve the worship it continues to receive."[41] He listed substantive shortcomings based on a weak research design and the distorted importance attached to single-parent families. Moynihan, he added, had not actually done systematic research for the report, nor was he trained for that task. His PhD was in International Relations, a "professional rather than a research-training program."[42] The report was originally intended as an internal document for policy makers, not publicly distributed social science research. The hagiography that was developing about the report in 2010 seemed to Gans to be both undeserved and connected to revived acrimony toward "unnamed liberals and social scientists who failed to do further research and writing on the failings of the Black family," a now familiar complaint reportedly voiced often by Moynihan and picked up by his more recent admirers.

Wilson's introduction to *The Truly Disadvantaged* pays repeated homage to Moynihan and lays out the scenario of his unfair treatment by long-haired radicals and black power bullies. Nearly the entire spectrum of social science research, from inflamed leftists to timid liberals, is excoriated by Wilson. The critics were viciously unfair and the rest were cowardly, willing to abdicate their social and scholarly responsibilities to avoid personal controversy. Moynihan was a prophet who foresaw the collapse of family stability, who dared to shine a light on the dysfunctional child rearing that took place in inner-city black ghettos, and who had been pilloried for his honesty and foresight. Wilson lamented the effects of this history on the state of urban policy research: "However, the controversy surrounding the Moynihan report had the effect of curtailing serious research on minority problems in the inner city for over a decade, as liberal scholars shied away from researching behavior construed as unflattering or stigmatizing to particular racial minorities."[43]

This rendering of an episode in intellectual history during the 1960s and beyond has gained wide acceptance among contemporary urban scholars. Douglas Massey and Robert Sampson, writing in 2009, characterized the story as follows: "Imagine Moynihan's shock and dismay upon finding himself the target of a vicious campaign of demonization by erstwhile friends in the liberal media and academia. . . . A more important legacy is what others concluded from the reaction it garnered. Having seen what happened to a well-known liberal who had in good faith tackled a sensitive issue from a well-grounded social scientific perspective, people could not help but conclude that addressing combustible racial issues was a dangerous enterprise."[44]

They then reprint a similar statement by Massey from 1995 when he defended both Moynihan and Oscar Lewis: "Object lessons were made of Oscar Lewis and Daniel Patrick Moynihan, and after the treatment these two prominent social scientists received, no one could miss the point. . . . The calumny heaped on these two distinguished social scientists had a chilling effect on social science over the next two decades."[45]

This is a "just-so" story about a contested area of policy research that has been told and retold by countless researchers and commentators, with almost no attention to whether it is an accurate account of what transpired.[46] The initial persecution of Moynihan, followed by the craven retreat from truth seeking by witnesses to his treatment, is a fable that underpins the revisionist account of Moynihan's contributions to poverty knowledge and his relevance for understanding current levels of poverty and social inequality. What are the facts behind this narration? Were Moynihan's critics vicious and unfair? Was his work underrated? Were scholars intimidated from emulating him, or did they just not agree with his theory, research, or conclusions?

The assertion that scholars stopped doing research on culture and poverty is impossible to verify, but seems dubious. No one is ever cited who claims deliberate avoidance of the topic for fear of criticism. The allegedly vicious critics are typically nameless. Research and publication on these issues certainly continued through the 1970s and '80s; if anything the topic received heightened attention. In *Freedom Is Not Enough*, Patterson cites an informed estimate that Moynihan's report "helped unleash a virtual avalanche of scholarship, as well as a torrent of public acrimony" amounting to "more than fifty books and five hundred journal articles [between 1965 and 1980 that] addressed the effects of poverty and discrimination on black families."[47] Elijah Anderson was doing inner-city ethnography with a cultural slant in the 1970s (e.g., *A Place on the Corner*, 1976).[48] John Ogbu, who along with Signithia Fordham, advanced the notion of fear of "acting white," was doing research on cultural differences between African American and nonwhite immigrant students during the 1970s and '80s.[49] Stanley Lieberson was writing comparative history of white immigrants and African Americans (*A Piece of the Pie*, 1980). Michael Harrington wrote a 1984 update of his classic study, titling this one *The New American Poverty*, in which he defended although disagreed with Moynihan, and engaged the issue of whether culture or external opportunity have the greatest impact. Michael Katz published *The Undeserving Poor* in 1989. Frances Fox Piven and her late husband/coauthor, Richard Cloward, published numerous books and articles about poverty and race throughout the period, and there were others. Some but not all of the foregoing authors were critical of Moynihan or Oscar Lewis, or both, but there were others, like Edward Banfield at Harvard, whose *The Unheavenly City* (1970) indicts the morals and behavior of poor people in cities.[50]

There was frequent and occasionally acrid disagreement over the different positions that scholars held, but the image of some kind of Stalinist campaign against Moynihan does not seem to fit the evidence. Nor were the writings of Moynihan's critics in the immediate aftermath, or in the years to follow, particularly unfriendly. Rainwater and Yancey's 1967 documentation of the report contains reprints of most of the early critics, including their own gentle criticism. There is passion and indignation in some of the entries, but most are careful and respectful, avoiding any kind of *ad hominem* accusations. As Gans pointed out after reviewing his own reaction forty-five years later, there were legitimate reasons to criticize the report. The campaign to resurrect the Moynihan Report, to lionize his work and vilify his critics, seems disproportional.

Moynihan retired from the Senate in 2001 and died in 2003. Especially in the aftermath of his death, there has been an outpouring of attention to, and reinvigoration of, his ideas and general theory about the causes and perpetuation of poverty. W. J. Wilson has been a leading figure in this effort, but many other high-level academic and governmental *personae* have joined in praise of Moynihan's landmark study. In 2007 the American Academy of Social and Political Science inaugurated the annual Daniel Patrick Moynihan Prize, created "to recognize social scientists and other leaders in the public arena who champion the use of informed judgment to advance the public good." High-level conferences were organized to discuss the merits and influence of this work. In 2009 the *Annals of the American Academy of Social and Political Science* devoted an entire issue to the influence of the Moynihan Report. In 2010 this same eminent journal published an issue on the topic of culture and poverty, with ubiquitous references to Moynihan. In 2013 the Urban Institute released a special report entitled "The Moynihan Report Revisited." The preponderance of these offerings praised him as a courageous scholar whose prescient thoughts about poverty hold valuable insights into the escalating distress of our current social condition. The view that poor people's dysfunctional culture is a root cause of their predicament draws from apparently impeccable academic authority.

The articles included in the *Annals* issue celebrating the Moynihan Report contain a great deal of solid research, and in several cases offer findings that contradict the report's basic conclusions. However, the introduction written by Robert Sampson and Douglass Massey (well-regarded researchers in the field of urban studies) is slanted in describing the report and contains some notable inaccuracies.[51] There is no hint of criticism of Moynihan, nor any suggestion that his research was wanting in any way. His critics are dismissed as shameless ideologues. The only one named is William Ryan, author of *Blaming the Victim*. He is identified as a "journalist," when he was actually a psychologist on the faculty of the Harvard Medical School. Mention of other critics was caricatures: "Young black militants and newly self-aware feminists joined in the rising tide of vilification, and Moynihan was widely pilloried not only as a racist, but a sexist to boot. A great irony is that few of his vociferous critics had actually read the document. It was still an internal document with a very limited number of copies."[52]

Actually, according to Rainwater and Yancey, demand was so immediate for copies of the report that in August of 1965 (less than a month after it was leaked), the Government Accounting Office printed and bound five hundred copies (for forty-five cents each). They sold out immediately and more were printed.[53] Gans makes it clear that he had a full copy of the report when he wrote his initial response. Massey and Sampson incorrectly cite Rainwater and Yancey as authorities for the assertion that these were unavailable until 1967. These are minor discrepancies, but not small points. The implication is to vilify the alleged vilifiers, and to exaggerate the quality of Moynihan's work and ideas.

His most critical thesis was that broken families instill the habits of poverty in their children, and that this inappropriate socialization is a primary reason poverty persists and grows. Moynihan repeated this concept often in his report, but the evidence was weak, a matter of correlations among variables. The one exception was his scissors finding, discussed earlier. Massey and Sampson do not mention this measure or the reported finding, even though Moynihan believed it was very important. Wilson, however, did include discussion of the scissors finding in his *Annals* article: "Like Oscar Lewis, Moynihan relates cultural patterns to structural factors and then discusses how these patterns come to influence other aspects of behavior. For example, in the concluding chapter of his report, he states that the situation of the black family 'may indeed have begun to feed on itself.'"[54]

Wilson went on to explain Moynihan's discovery that the long trend of positive correlation between unemployment and welfare enrollments was reversed in the early 1960s, suggesting to him that dependency had taken hold. Wilson then quoted the statement by Alice O'Connor, reprinted earlier, that "Moynihan sealed the argument that the 'pathology' had become self-perpetuating." However, as noted earlier, O'Connor proceeded to explain why he was wrong in his interpretation of this confounded result. Her next sentence is: "The fact is that the statistical correlation 'proved' nothing of the sort."[55] This highly relevant clause was omitted in Wilson's rendering of what she said. Worse, as mentioned, Wilson and Neckerman's own earlier analyses of employment, welfare, and marriage data had refuted the validity of the scissors interpretation.

Contemporary defenders of Moynihan protest too much about his critics, and too easily ignore his shortcomings. The importance of including a cultural element in explaining poverty, especially within inner-city African American neighborhoods, seems to have outweighed usual cautions in assessing research quality. A contest between culture and structure has been drawn in the debate over poverty's causes: conservatives opt for culture as a proxy that blames personal characteristics of poor people; leftists blame the exploitative and racist structure of the economy, including housing segregation and inequitable employment opportunities. The mainstream tries to include both elements in an allegedly balanced approach. The structure imposes disadvantages, but individuals damage themselves by making bad choices; poverty outcomes derive from both. The ultimate question is, what causes which? Are broken families the dependent or independent variable? Does marital instability result from unfair job opportunities for young black men? Or, do female-headed households nurture children who become unemployable? Do neighborhoods of low-cost housing consign children to substandard schools and exposure to dangers, or do the defective norms and values of poor families gathered into neighborhoods create criminogenic environments? In terms of both theory and policy, these questions matter. And they are the crux of the argument between Moynihan's defenders and his critics, historical and contemporary.

Wilson, Sampson, and a host of colleagues and students have undertaken very ambitious and sophisticated research programs, using panel studies and large data sets to examine the interrelationships among variables and the extent to which exogenous (structural) and endogenous (cultural) factors are associated with poverty and other negative indicators. Although they posit dual causality, there is a lopsided emphasis on the behavioral characteristics of poor mothers, their partners, and children. The structural impediments, like insufficient employment and substandard schools, are presented as givens, whereas the personal circumstances are viewed as being somehow tractable. If individuals would try harder to postpone and manage childbirth, or work harder in school, or keep their marriages together, then they could overcome the obstacles embedded in the structure that surrounds them.

The research that emerged from the controversy over the Moynihan Report has diverged among academics in directions that reflect shifting politics over the five decades since its release. Canons of evidence and standards of research practice should be important arbiters of accuracy and validity of research findings, but the nature of arguments and the political implications of explanations that researchers pursue have had considerable influence on the acceptance of research findings in policies and programs. Research on very low-income families and the challenges facing their children has continued along pathways sketched in this chapter. In the next chapter, I examine the research and controversies surrounding low-income families, especially African Americans living in conditions of concentrated poverty.

3

Kinship and Family Structure

• • • • • • • • • • • • • • • • •

Ethnocentric Myopia

> The role of the family in shaping character and ability is so pervasive as to be easily overlooked. The family is the basic social unit of American life; it is the basic socializing unit. By and large, adult conduct in society is learned as a child.
> —D. P. Moynihan, *The Report on the Negro Family*

The presumed importance of "traditional" patriarchal families was the core of Moynihan's analysis; nuclear families with strong male authority were essential. A man in charge of provisioning and decision making, and a wife in charge of children and domestic management, together comprising a functioning unit of civil existence and social reproduction. In the 1960s numerous associations were drawn between this demographic shift and indicators of social and individual distress. Unemployment, educational failure, poverty, and delinquency were all regarded as outcomes of a deficient child-rearing system—conditions believed to be caused more by inappropriate parenting than racism or external economic factors. This chain of logic shaped the emphasis on family structure over opportunity structure in Moynihan's policy analysis. African American family structure was interpreted as a unique product of residual influences of slavery and discrimination, culturally different and disadvantaged in comparison with white middle-class family patterns.

Reprising the family structure argument for poverty has been a primary feature in the rehabilitation of Moynihan's legacy since the 1980s. This is an intricate maneuver, however, that requires ignoring several obstinate errors in both Moynihan's analysis and that of his contemporary supporters. First is the problem of cultural distinctiveness. Moynihan focused on African American poverty and the defective family structure he believed was associated with that ethnicity, giving scant attention to class differences. For reasons of history, persecution, and social isolation he posited that African American culture favored a "matriarchal" family structure that was at odds with success: "Ours is a society which presumes male leadership in private and public affairs. The arrangements of society facilitate such leadership and reward it. A subculture, such as that of the Negro American, in which this is not the pattern, is placed at a distinct disadvantage."[1]

Moynihan evidently had some knowledge about variation in kinship systems, an obsessive interest of anthropologists in that period, but his ideas were crudely out of sync with their structural functional analysis, which examined this variation within a framework of cultural relativism. Kinship was regarded as elementary in human functioning, the key to evolutionary success; every culture has had some form of marriage and a system for counting, labeling, and mobilizing relatives. Nowhere, however, has there ever been a "matriarchal" society or culture. This term, which Moynihan used so freely to describe the family structure of African Americans, is an empty set, the theoretical mirror image of male authority, a governance system that evidently never existed and still does not. Chief among the early (and later) critics of Moynihan's thesis were feminists who argued persuasively that black women wield even less power and are paid worse wages than black men, and deemed his presumption that only men should make decisions to be sexist claptrap. Patriarchy was not the natural state, even if matriarchy was nonexistent.[2]

Anthropologists had uncovered considerable variation in the extent of influence women exert under different types of kinship systems. Matrilineality, a system where descent is reckoned through female lines but authority still resides with men, is sometimes confused with "matriarchy." Structurally it does confer greater influence on the women in households and kin groups. The celebrated example is the League of the Iroquois, a once powerful confederacy of six related matrilineal Indian tribes in upper New York state and Canada. Women of the clans were instrumental in selecting leaders and deliberating matters of war and diplomacy, but they did not lead or fight. As a general principle, in matrilineal systems children belong to the clan and household of their mothers, making divorce more easily achieved for unhappy wives, compared with patrilineal systems where custody of children would be lost to the husband's family.

Worldwide studies of kinship have offered a panoply of cultural strategies for securing sustenance, warding off danger, and managing procreation. Associations can be drawn between subsistence and kinship organization, between politics and marriage alliances, between collective control of resources and tribal systems of kinship. Some kinship systems reckon relatedness based on female lines of descent, others along male lines; still others count relatives on both sides. There have been many combinations of descent and residence and degrees of paternal authority. By the 1960s anthropologists had demonstrated conclusively that patriarchal nuclear families were not the dominant choice among earth's billions of humans and the myriad ecological conditions they inhabit. Moynihan's belief that this family type was the only possible route to success was both ethnocentric and naive. Belief that female-headed families were a cultural choice among African Americans, a signature of their social distinctiveness, was similarly ethnocentric and naive. Anthropologists had identified a somewhat universal tendency for poor people to avoid legalized marriage, entering instead into what are labeled "consensual unions." Marriage is costly and entails obligations that may be too onerous. Men leave their families when they cannot find work at home, and sometimes they never return, a pattern that can be found across a wide range of geography and culture. Such behaviors are mostly driven by economic need and scarcely are confined to African Americans, a very heterogeneous and expansive demographic category speciously defined as "racial."

"Prescient" is a term of praise monotonously invoked to describe Moynihan's report. He sounded the bell early in warning about the collapse of families and concomitant rise in poverty. He singled out fatherless families as the major problem facing African Americans, and presented them as the self-replicating crucible of persistent failure. In the decades that followed this prophecy, the rates of female-headed families and nonmarital children (formerly called "illegitimate") had skyrocketed. In 2010, 73 percent of African American children were born outside of marriage, compared with 53 percent of Hispanics and 29 percent of non-Hispanic whites. These are large discrepancies that would seem to confirm that African Americans have a worse problem with family stability. However, the twenty-year rates of change on these measures tell a slightly different story. Between 1990 and 2010 the rate of nonmarital childbearing increased 12 percent for African Americans, 51 percent for Hispanics, and 61 percent for non-Hispanic whites.[3] The sharpest rises for all three groups occurred after 2008, when poverty and unemployment spiked in response to a massive recession. Moynihan incorrectly believed that African Americans practiced a different and disabling form of kinship that was intensifying their poverty independent of external opportunities and limits. The current situation, in which increased numbers of female-headed families are found across the ethnic spectrum and in clear association with failures and changes in the economy, would seem to invalidate rather than vindicate Moynihan's original prediction. The primacy of family structure as a cause of poverty, rather than merely a consequence, was the essence of Moynihan's argument. Something needed to be done to repair the fragile families of impoverished African Americans. He claimed that their families were different from those in other groups, and they were specifically in need of guidance to adopt middle class practices as a prelude to achieving economic stability.

Several questions raised by this issue could be resolved, or at least addressed. First, what are African American families like? Moynihan's rendition was based on census data and secondary sources. How accurate were his deductions? Second, what is the relationship between male unemployment and female-headed households? To what extent is this pattern a culturally neutral response to economic pressures on marriage? Finally, what factors uniquely affect African American marriage stability and the rate of nonmarital child rearing? Much existing data is relevant to these questions, both quantitative and qualitative, most of it unavailable at the time Moynihan was writing his report.

All Our Kin

The Moynihan Report stimulated a spate of inquiries into the essential character of black families in poor neighborhoods. Hannerz and Liebow described familial relations of the men they studied on separate street corners in Washington, DC. Their descriptions of detached fathering and frequent tensions in love relationships bore similarities to Moynihan's version. Even so, ethnography added depth and texture to these relationships, and linked their troubles more directly to the problem of finding work that paid enough to support a family, rather than cultural license to be irresponsible. Carol Stack's 1974 monograph titled *All Our Kin: Strategies for Survival in a Black Community*[4] provided a more fulsome view of kinship in and among impoverished black households in the urban Midwest. As mentioned earlier, Stack attended the same graduate program in which Oscar Lewis taught; he was a member of her doctoral committee. He invited her to breakfast one morning to meet Pat Moynihan and eavesdrop on his and Moynihan's conversation about culture and poverty. Although she was not part of the discussion, Carol was at the same moment contemplating her dissertation fieldwork around those very same issues. In 1968 she embarked on an extended stay in an unnamed city in Illinois, in a black working-class neighborhood she called the Flats. She was interested in "urban poverty and the 'domestic strategies' of urban-born black Americans whose parents had migrated from the South to the Flats."[5]

Her own strategy was to become friends with the people she hoped to understand, to gain slowly a perspective on their lives from their own point of view. She began by focusing on a single large extended family who had successively migrated out of Arkansas to St. Louis, the Flats, and Chicago. The pathways and resources that enabled this organized dispersion were viewed through links in a family chain that was both fluid and efficacious. This network emerged in Stack's analysis as a different way of conceptualizing family relations, a broadly structured adaptation to adversity not unlike kinship organization in other settings where men may be missing or marriage is difficult. Moynihan's bleak picture of young unmarried mothers struggling in isolation was revised to include the larger landscape of grandparents, parents, siblings, aunts, uncles, children's fathers and kin, fictive kin, and partners of family members—access to whose aid and advice helped ease the burdens of parenting. Trading and gifting constituted an informal economy that redistributed small surpluses and coped with minor emergencies. Frequent exchanges formed a social glue that amplified the importance of family and facilitated survival under conditions of extreme privation.

Stack argued that designating such families as "disorganized" ignores the existence of an effective architecture of sharing and connectedness. As most anthropologists of that era would have done in a community ethnography, she charted and analyzed the rules and alignments of kin ties among the families she had gotten to know in the Flats. Her positioning was unique, however, and the timing of her work was highly significant. Stack's portrait offered a jarring contradiction with Moynihan's, a response to the pejorative treatment of black family relations. The characters in her ethnography faced unsolvable financial problems, the worst effects of which were mitigated by trading and sharing among a wide group of kin. This formation is shaped differently from the conventional two-parent nuclear family; Stack presents it as an adaptive alternative configuration. Where others had asserted disorganization and dysfunction, Stack presented evidence of organized strategic actions. Spreading disadvantage around did not eliminate the underlying problem, and not all emergencies could be handled, but the preponderance of family ties that she observed were helpful, not aggravators of poverty or mechanisms of self-replicating failure. The problem, Stack concluded in agreement with virtually every other thoughtful writer on this topic, was not enough jobs. In the Flats, neither men nor women could find jobs that paid enough to give children what they needed.

Stack's account, which was extremely well written and widely read, commanded attention and added new challenges to the thesis that broken families cause poverty, especially among African Americans. Other work from that period and beyond also focused on resilience and adaptive creativity in black families. In 1975 Joyce Aschenbrenner, an anthropologist who worked on a larger study of American kinship by Raymond T. Smith and David Schneider, published a monograph about black kinship in Chicago (*Lifelines: Black Families in Chicago*) that strongly confirmed Stack's analysis.[6]

Joyce Ladner, a black sociologist, did a study of poor young black women, an account with a message similar to Stack's, conducted in and around the infamous Pruitt-Igoe housing project in St. Louis. Her work was part of a general rebellion against pathologizing black culture by white sociology.[7] Shifting attention to the pathological features of white middle-class values and behavior, Ladner celebrated the virtues of "soul," the courage and creativity of victims forging humanity within an inhumane system. Her model of thought was anticolonial, part of the global decolonization going on at the time. She argued that black women and families should not be viewed in comparison to white values and ideals, but rather within the context of their own history and culture. Ladner criticized Frazier and Moynihan for deracinating African American culture, disapprovingly quoting Glazer and Moynihan, who had written in *Beyond the Melting Pot*, "It is not possible for Negroes to view themselves as other ethnic groups viewed themselves because . . . the Negro is only an American and nothing else. He has no values and culture to guard and protect."[8] Ladner strongly disagreed, arguing that a long history of discrimination and deprivation, orchestrated by the practitioners of white culture, had filtered through the timeless memory of African ancestors and produced an adaptive system that has been vilified instead of celebrated, adding insult to the injury of enslavement and Jim Crow.

During the 1970s there was a florescence of oppositional versions of black history and culture. Andrew Billingsley, a sociologist at Howard University, critiqued the maltreatment of black children by the welfare establishment (*Children of the Storm*, 1972) and examined the challenges facing black families (*Black Families in White America*, 1968), as well as celebrating the survival skills and creative humanity of black culture. Robert Hill, then research director for the Urban League, compiled a study entitled *The Strengths of Black Families* in 1972.[9] Billingsley wrote in the foreword to Hill's book: "One question that arises immediately is why has so much attention been given in the literature and most media to the problems Black families face and so little attention to the heroic nature of their grappling with these problems?"[10] New perspectives on black families emphasizing strengths and adaptive capacities gained acceptance, but the subject remained contentious. Conservative supporters of Moynihan's thesis maintained that this was just ideological defensiveness and ethnic chauvinism, and these alleged strengths were based on weak and selective evidence.

There was a subtle distinction between Oscar Lewis's use of the concept of "adaptation" and the meaning put forth by Stack, Hill, Billingsley, Ladner, and Aschenbrenner. Lewis viewed adaptations as responses to impinging conditions (poverty in this case), a set of compensatory behaviors and norms designed to ease the misery of the moment, but that could actually make things worse in the long run. Stack's analysis finds greater equilibrium in the precarious but successful maintenance of critical lines of support, the vital lifelines also described by others. Family is not the household, but rather the kin-based unit of adaptation, where flexible inclusion of members, personal attachments and incentives, and access to distributional resources offer both an emotional buffer and a hand up. The difference in interpretation lies in whether the alternative family structure is blamed for lack of material success (O. Lewis and Moynihan), or that profoundly unequal material conditions are made less bleak through creative cooperation among kinfolk (Stack, Aschenbrenner, Ladner).

The Way We Never Were

Responses to Moynihan raised the issue of which culture is more pathological, black or white? The bad attitudes and misbehavior of white people in America were not hard to demonstrate. Who, after all, was responsible for the orgy of lynching that had continued in the South until after World War II? The term *race riot* had previously referred to roaming mobs of white people who would enter black neighborhoods during tense moments and commit random acts of violence and destruction. Who raped and plundered Native Americans as part of worldwide colonial brigandage inflicted by Europeans on nonwhite peoples? White middle-class values and family patterns were being held up as the ideal against which black families were found wanting. Some critics found that comparison to be risible and the height of obfuscation. Stephanie Coontz, a historian specializing in family studies, serves up a feast of contradictions in our images of the "traditional family" and the realities of historical and contemporary domestic relations in the US.[11] Child labor, corporal punishment, limited education for children (especially girls), the impunity of wife abuse and infidelity, legal powerlessness of women, early death and desertion of spouses, stingy charities, and an uncaring state were all part of the landscape of normal family relations in the early twentieth century. The 1960s was a time of myth-making about families on TV. *Father Knows Best, Leave It to Beaver*, and the *Donna Reed Show* were about prosperous middle-class white TV families who coped weekly with comical and usually trivial problems with aplomb, wisdom, and warmth. At the same time, the suburban reality of families like the Cleavers and the Nelsons was more ambivalent and complicated. The suburbs, which sucked all the federal resources out of cities, were built for families like these—white, middle-class, upwardly mobile—but the isolation of single-family tract developments also posed new challenges to communal and social life. The relative affluence of that existence served up personal contradictions. Frequently mentioned was concern about bored wives with too many household conveniences and too much time to kill, who took too many tranquilizers and drank too much.

In contrast with the bored housewife of the suburbs, black mothers in inner cities were presented as greedy, lazy, and ignorant—producing out-of wedlock children to qualify for more welfare. Moynihan's concern with "dependency," the quality he seized on in his scissors finding, was integral to the pejorative image of African American culture, the root of the tangle of pathology. The "welfare queen" trope that served Ronald Reagan so admirably in cutting social programs in the 1980s was nurtured in the 1960s and strengthened by Moynihan. Charles Murray's 1984 rendition of this phenomenon argued that welfare caused dependency and encouraged illegitimacy and bad parenting. Wilson and Neckerman (1987) demonstrated conclusively in chapter 4 of *The Truly Disadvantaged* that the causal link between welfare receipt and either family breakups or nonmarital births was nonexistent. It is noteworthy in that regard that after drastic cuts and the transformation of welfare in the 1990s, when dependency was abruptly curtailed, the rates of nonmarital births and female-headed households have continued to climb.

Moynihan wrote at a time when Freudian ideas about gender roles and children were seriously regarded. The influence of psychology on the general argument about families and child rearing was reflected in Moynihan's analysis. Two well-known psychologists, Erik Erikson and Thomas Pettigrew, offered Freudian opinions that black males raised by their mothers experienced deep-seated problems. Pettigrew was quoted in the report: "Embittered by their experiences with men, many Negro mothers often act to perpetuate the mother-centered pattern by taking a greater interest in their daughters than their sons."[12] Their work provided much of the authority for Moynihan's belief in the pathological character of female-headed households and the rectitude of his ideas about patriarchy. More generally, however, the roles of women were changing in a sometimes confusing manner. Affluent mothers who worked outside the home were criticized for neglecting their children, but those who stayed home were sometimes labeled as "schizophrenogenic," possessive hens who hovered over their children, creating multiple neuroses in them. Poor mothers who did not work but received welfare instead, were excoriated for laziness and dependency, and also condemned for inadequate parenting and failing to provide children with a work ethic. Women who were too emotional about their male children were thought to be causing them to be effeminate and weak; those who were more restrained were charged with withholding affection and causing personality damage that way. Homosexuality was viewed as a result of bad mothering, or the absence of a strong male role model, or both.[13]

Out of this welter of contradictory and mystified thought was a singular belief in the importance of a well-balanced, two-parent, nuclear family with sufficient income to permit the mother to stay home and provide children with constant guidance and all basic emotional needs. Against this image, divorce, infidelity, the conflict between personal pleasure and familial responsibility, and uncertainties about how children should be disciplined, were all part of the confusing aura of uneven prosperity and concocted nostalgia about family values. Impoverished black families where single women shouldered the burdens of child rearing and provisioning, often through receipt of public welfare, and whose children did poorly in school and were likely to be arrested for delinquency, posed a stark contrast with the idealized image of the prosperous, happy, and stable two-parent family, even if that reality was somewhat rare in any sector of US society.

As controversy continued over the character of African American kinship, the rates of single parenting and nonmarital births continued to rise sharply in the 1970s and '80s for African Americans, but with similar trend lines for Hispanic and non-Hispanic whites. Rates for all three groups rose in tandem during the 1990s, with especially sharp increases after 2007. The synchronous growth in this phenomenon for all three ethnic segments implicates factors in the underlying economy, like jobs. It is hard to start married life with no income, but sex continues and hence come babies. The unemployment rate spiked from 6 percent to 10 percent in the same period that nonmarital childbearing was on the rise. The black-white disparity in unemployment rates remained large and stable during that period, at about 10 percent higher for blacks. In 2010 white male unemployment stood at 6 percent, whereas the black male rate was 17 percent; in 1980 it had been 8 percent vs. 18 percent, with approximately the same difference at intervals in between. Altogether, these data indicate that fluctuations of the economy and employment have much to do with shifts in the frequency of marriage, and that for more than four decades black men have experienced a large and constant disadvantage in gaining employment.

Marriage Pools

A simple theory about low marriage rates among African Americans is that there is a scarcity of suitable male spouses caused by high rates of unemployment and incarceration among young black men. This is an empirical question, based on the assumption that women prefer marital partners with jobs and without criminal records. W. J. Wilson was among the first to focus on this dimension. He explained this idea at length in *The Truly Disadvantaged*: "The high percentages of out-of-wedlock births and female-headed households can be directly tied to the labor-market status of black males. As we have documented, black women, especially young black women, are facing a shrinking pool of 'marriageable' (i.e., economically stable) men."[14]

If the supply of mates is not evenly divided between the sexes, that disparity would explain a lot about failure to marry.[15] As mentioned, the jobless rate for black men has been consistently worse than for whites of similar ages; older teen males have faced the worst joblessness (recently exceeding 50 percent in many places), with a gap between them and comparable white males that grew considerably between 1960 and 1980. During the 1980s, when Wilson was calling attention to worsening inner-city conditions, the incidence of black nonmarital childbearing was increasing along with the growing rate of young black male joblessness. In 1985, among those aged between twenty and twenty-four, Wilson calculated that there were fewer than forty-five eligible males per hundred females.[16] In that same year, only about 35 percent of black women were married. The next two decades brought unprecedented levels of incarceration, especially of young black males. In 1985 fewer than 10 percent of black men had spent time in prison; by 2010 the rate had grown to 16 percent.[17] These two factors among men, being jobless or in jail, have shrunk the marriage pool drastically for black women. By 2010 only 25 percent of black women were married; for whites it was just over 50 percent, and it was 42 percent for Hispanics. All ethnic categories had increased proportions of unmarried women, but the gap between black and white remained very large.

Two factors were at work in directing these processes. The labor market had undergone marked changes that accelerated during the 1980s and continued thereafter. Manufacturing jobs were steadily disappearing, and a large and growing number of women entered the workforce.

Deindustrialization and adverse trade agreements like the North American Free Trade Act (NAFTA) drained jobs for low-skilled workers, especially from northern and midwestern cities where African Americans had migrated out of the South. An attack on labor unions commenced during the first month of Ronald Reagan's presidency and inflicted sustained, steady losses, especially in the private sector. The post–World War II rise of labor unions in the United States had been a major reason that so many industrial workers had been able to ascend into the middle class. The decline in union membership from 1980 to 2011 tracks almost exactly the growing decline in middle-class incomes.[18] These wage reductions, and the gains of the women's movement, also signaled the second shift in the composition of the labor force, with the mass entry of women into jobs at all levels. Income losses in working-class families were compensated by adding the wages of wives; the two-earner household became the norm and a necessity. Single-earner households were typically headed by women, whose earnings were lower than men's. Welfare legislation in 1996 pushed another large cohort of low-skilled women into jobs that paid little better than welfare and created an even tighter squeeze on employment at the bottom. At higher income levels, reduced gender discrimination and increased educational opportunities allowed greater autonomy for dissatisfied middle-class wives to leave their husbands and still be able to support themselves and young children. Employment opportunities for men that offer adequate remuneration have been deemed the most important factor in maintaining strong marriages. Changes in that sphere brought collateral losses in family stability for many Americans, but especially for low-income African Americans.

Frank Furstenberg, a sociologist specializing in family studies, has assembled strong evidence that the patterns of nonmarital childbearing between black and white women have become quite similar within lower income groups, and that the incidence of pregnancy among both black and white teens has dropped as well.[19] He chides Moynihan for not seeing the class distinctions that were evident in 1965 and contends that his emphasis on race created a false trail of causation: subsequent trends have proved that "it is insufficient to have strong cultural values about marriages if the economic and social conditions that foster marriage are not maintained."[20] For black men in particular, the economic conditions favoring marriage became steadily worse over the period in question, even worse than for other working-class men whose wages and job security had deteriorated.

Causes of Black Male Unemployment

African American men occupy a difficult position in the labor force. Ste-
reotypic images of black men are even more loaded and negative than
those attached to their female counterparts, who are often depicted as
"welfare queens" and "crack whores." Black men are portrayed as lazy, volatile, oversexed, undisciplined, undereducated, and inclined to criminality.[21]
These characteristics are not compatible with success in the labor market.
Despite laws against it, outright discrimination in hiring is rampant and is
rationalized by economists under a concept known as "statistical discrimination." This refers to employers' practice of generalizing from presumed
knowledge about an ethnic group to individual applicants, disqualifying
members of the disfavored group, thus (again presumably) raising the statistical likelihood of hiring someone who will work out. Hiring decisions,
especially for low-skilled jobs, are fraught with uncertainty. Under the
terms of statistical discrimination, race is a covertly acceptable disqualifier,
based on belief in stereotypes or previous experience with other individuals of a particular group. A decision not to hire an apparently qualified
black applicant can be based on unrelated experience with someone else of
the same color, or simply the global conviction that black men have a poor
work ethic: "The continuing significance of race in the minds of employers
has been demonstrated in numerous contexts. Interviews with employers
reveal the persistence of strong negative associations with minority workers, with particularly negative characteristics attributed to African American men."[22] In a large recent study of applications for entry-level jobs, the
rate of interviews and offers to equally qualified black applicants was half
that of whites. Equally qualified black men with no criminal records fared
worse than white men recently released from prison.[23] These obstacles,
which can only be described as sanctioned racism, are well established in
this line of research but little questioned.

The 2009 special issue of the *Annals of the American Academy of Political
and Social Sciences* dedicated to "revisiting" the Moynihan Report contains
two articles about the employment problems of black men in the United
States that shed much light and raise important questions.[24] Moynihan's
initial concern was employment; he worked for the US Department of
Labor when he wrote his report. He recognized that the inability of African
American men to compete in the job market was the main factor under-
mining their ability to marry. He placed blame for that problem somewhat

equally on discrimination by employers and the unsuitability of black workers due to inappropriate family and neighborhood socialization. Employer responsibility remained nebulous, however, and he focused instead on problems with the job seekers. Discrimination was treated as a natural condition, like gravity or weather, rather than considered as a specific part of the problem. Devah Pager and Diana Karafin examined both attitudes and experiences of New York City employers of entry-level workers. Their goal was to ascertain employers' general beliefs about black applicants and to gather descriptions of their past experiences with black workers. How prejudiced are the people who make hiring decisions for unskilled entry-level jobs? Do positive or negative experiences with black workers affect general beliefs about the employability of black men?

The respondents were predominantly male (70 percent) and majority white (59 percent) managers of small and chain retail stores, services, and restaurants. Those who spoke of shortcomings or defects of black workers (60 percent) closely matched the size of the white segment of the sample (59 percent), although the authors do not break this down. The comments that are reproduced range from banal to virulent. "They don't want to work—you can tell by the attitude, clothing, the general body language." "Just being lazy and not wanting to work." "Maybe they think that this country owes them so much. Because of slavery and all that . . . feel like they deserve something . . . [so] they don't want to work." "Unfortunately we've bred generations of welfare . . . a lot of these people just don't have any work values."[25] In addition to complaints about a lack of work ethic, respondents also criticized clothing, attitude, speech, and likelihood of criminal tendencies, using language similar in lack of subtlety to that reproduced above. All of these comments were generalizations about young black males, racial lore. When respondents were asked to recount experiences, both negative and positive, with African American employees, it brought forth anecdotes of both varieties, although more positive or neutral than negative. In one case, the employer told of a black woman he hired and subsequently grew to dislike, which caused him to be leery of all black applicants thereafter. In other cases involving positive experiences, employers did not alter their views of black workers in general, but rather indicated that their black employees were exceptional cases. Pager and Karafin conclude that a great many employers hold deeply rooted stereotypes that are a serious disadvantage to black job seekers. These findings mirror those of several previous larger quantitative studies. However, their other result, that personal experiences do not shake these prejudices, gives added reason for concern. "This analysis holds potentially troubling implications for hiring behavior. We know from the results of field experiments that employers consistently avoid black workers, hiring them at roughly half the rate of equally qualified whites. Where models of statistical discrimination might interpret this behavior as the rational response to observed differences in the productivity of black and white workers, the present research questions this conclusion."[26]

These findings are very strong evidence that the biggest problems facing black job seekers are the entrenched attitudes of white employers who believe they make bad workers, even when actual experiences with black workers have produced contrary results. These are not rational beliefs, certainly not when applied to individuals who offer good qualifications. Whether one calls this "statistical" racism, or just the old-fashioned kind that feeds on fear and loathsome stereotypes, its large significance in preventing access of black youth to viable positions in the workforce should be regarded as "cultural" behavior by employers that causes needless poverty and hardship. It is also worth noting that hiring decisions made under the auspices of statistical racism are more, not less, likely to be wrong because the pool of applicants has been narrowed and distorted irrationally. Suitable black applicants are gratuitously eliminated, while less qualified whites who could prove unsuccessful are more likely to be chosen instead.

The other article on black employment problems was written by Harry Holzer, a senior fellow at the Urban Institute and former chief economist for the Department of Labor. Holzer offered an "update" on Moynihan's ideas, which he labeled "stunningly prescient." As has been described already, labor conditions for young black men went from bad in 1965, to pretty terrible in 1985, to catastrophic in 2010. This persistent trajectory is the basis for validating the prescient qualities of Moynihan's perspective. He was right about the future problem, but was he right about what was causing it? Holzer recounted the tangle of pathology that begins with female-headed households, to which he added the unforeseen crack cocaine economy of the 1980s and 90s, as well as the staggering increase in incarceration of young black men beginning at about the same time. Welfare changes in 1996 brought added pressure: "While these women were pouring into the labor market, their male counterparts continued to pour out."[27]

Holzer's portrait is extremely pessimistic. He commented at length on the path from the alienation of black youth, which he believes is a consequence of growing up in a broken home in a poor neighborhood, to illegal alternatives to the lack of legal jobs, to the astounding rate of involvement by young black men in the criminal justice system. Citing another study, he claimed that "more than a third of all young black men are now incarcerated, on parole, or on probation at any point in time."[28] Although not fully embracing the explanation that family structure is to blame, he assigned it great weight in his discussion. He presented the problem as a cascade of effects of careless upbringing by underresourced and inexperienced single mothers, leading to children's delinquent behavior and educational failure, rendering most sons unemployable. The many hurdles that face ex-felons are also discussed. I will take up this issue in greater depth, but suffice to say that this is an extremely large issue affecting a widening circle of families and communities. In most states ex-felons lose the right to vote (either temporarily or permanently); cannot hold certain licenses, work in many occupations, or live in public housing; and are forbidden access to a wide variety of social supports and financial aid. They have great difficulty supporting themselves by legal means and are usually ill-equipped to support a family.

Marriage Promotion

Holzer called for reform of the barriers affecting ex-felons, and more investment in reentry and antirecidivism programs. Expanding the Earned Income Tax Credit was another suggestion. He recommended reexamining the impact of court-ordered child support policies. In the name of personal responsibility, states track down and seize the wages of fathers of dependent children who have received public benefits. Funds collected this way typically go straight back to the state, not to children or their mothers. These actions can take more than half a paycheck, deducted automatically. Holzer described this practice as a disincentive for low-skill and low-paid fathers to take any job in the legal economy. It is also a toxic element in family relationships. To qualify for assistance, mothers must identify fathers of their children. The state locates the fathers, garnishees their wages, and uses the restitution gained to pay back funds the state has already expended in aid to the family. A low-paid worker who can barely support himself loses much of his income; his children do not get the money that was taken, the state does. This policy, which must sound good to Republican audiences in town hall meetings, does not promote amicable or conciliatory relations between errant fathers and their kids, or their kids' mothers. Despite this and other punitive and contradictory practices, an official policy of the Bush II and Obama administrations has been marriage promotion—programs to encourage unmarried parents to get legal, and to help married couples in troubled relationships learn how to work out their problems, raise kids, and budget their finances. A great deal has been spent on these efforts (more than $100 million per year since 2005), and the yield is negligible.

"Poor couples don't get divorced because they're less adept at communication than couples with healthy 401(k)s and three-car garages. Poor people get divorced because they're poor, and being poor makes you stressed, and being stressed makes it harder for you to communicate, which makes is more likely that you'll split."[29] To the extent that stress over not having enough money is the main source of tension in marriages of poor couples, the standard marriage promotion effort aims purely at symptoms, not the cause. The typical format for marriage promotion consists of support groups and workshops designed to improve relationship skills through training in better communications, parenting, and what are called life skills. Sessions are funded in part by Temporary Assistance to Needy Families (TANF), and attendance at them can be tied to eligibility for other benefits. Attendance often does include small material inducements in meals, diapers, gift cards, cash honoraria, and networking, in addition to the educational value of the programs being offered. The length and reach of these programs, that have been offered in nearly all states through both Republican and Democratic administrations, yield sufficient data to begin determining the effectiveness of this approach. A recent article in the *Chronicle of Higher Education* (Jan. 20, 2014) titled "The Great Mom and Dad Experiment" reviewed the results of evaluation research on this topic.[30] Their short version is: "The federal government has spent nearly a billion dollars to help poor couples stay together—with almost nothing to show for it. So why aren't we pulling the plug?" The article cites a recent review of evidence by Matthew Johnson, director of the Marriage and Family Studies Laboratory at Binghamton University.[31] Evaluations have been published on several programs that indicate weak to no results from these interventions. In most settings, the program had no effect compared

with control groups; in some cases, the outcomes were worse for the experimental groups. The program in Florida showed that after three years,
couples had more instability and fathers were even less involved with their
children than those in the control group. Only a few programs showed
positive results, and these tended to disappear a few months following the
intervention.

Johnson claims that part of the problem is that the original program
designs were not based on evidence or reviewed for scientific soundness.
He also suggests that the whole marriage promotion enterprise might be
constructed on a set of spurious correlations: "Yet, despite numerous studies describing the association of marital status and satisfaction with all
manner of positive outcomes, it is not at all clear that there is a causal benefit to marriage."[32] Kathryn Edin, a sociologist who has done a great deal
of research on single mothers and fathers, and who has served as a consul-
tant on marriage promotion programs, objected in the *Chronicle* article to
Johnson's dismissal of program effects based on strictly quantitative data.
Her qualitative studies of how poor women survive, why they have babies
they cannot afford, and what roles are played by fathers of these babies have
contributed important insights into these issues.[33] Edin's involvement with
marriage promotion activities has led her to believe these services are valuable to struggling couples in ways that elude the statistical measures of success. Supporters of the concept cited in the *Chronicle* article compare this
program to Head Start, the popular federal preschool program that also
has produced weak evidence of closing achievement gaps in low-income
children. Nevertheless, there has been limited pressure to end Head Start.
Although initially justified as a school readiness program, recognition of
the importance of Head Start for low-income working mothers in need of
day care outweighs skepticism over mediocre results later in school.

Marriage assistance for struggling couples also may be a service that is
needed by some and provides help that is positive, even if it is not enough
to ensure stable unions or produce impressive outcome statistics. Poor
families face a meager and declining array of services that can provide
diapers, for example, or a chance to socialize and eat a free meal, or the
other small benefits that participation in marriage promotion programs
enables. However, the estimated cost of these programs is about $11,000
per couple. Instead, what might be the benefit of expanding the earned
income tax credit by that amount, or creating a separate family allowance
program, or some other direct transfer of substantial financial resources to

struggling couples with children? Although families derive some material benefit from the present arrangement, the value of those elements (about $200) is far below the $11,000 currently being spent.[34] The issue in debating marriage promotion programs that do not seem to have much effect on the problem that they were designed to solve should be, as the *Chronicle* article suggests, whether we are really getting $1 billion worth of value from these efforts. Evidence suggests we are not, and the reason may be, as Johnson speculates, that the original theory was wrong. Robust correlations between marital status and poverty have clouded both policy and programming. If incapable families are an outcome rather than a driver of poverty, then fixing families relies on ending poverty.

Moynihan's emphasis on families headed by unmarried women was the centerpiece of his argument, deliberately cloaked in race and not framed in terms of class. The statistics he relied on suffered from many weaknesses, and his capacity to interpret them was hobbled by his lack of expertise in that area and his ethnocentric view of families. In the troubled political and economic environment of the 1970s and '80s, his chosen indicator of pathology registered sharply increasing rates of nonmarital child rearing, a condition he seemingly blamed more on the alleged moral lassitude of the 1960s than the punitive policies of Nixon and Reagan. Increases were greatest among African Americans, and poverty rates in this segment continued to be much higher than the national average, but people with low incomes regardless of ethnicity were also experiencing a rise in female-headed families. Bad parenting emerged as the consensus explanation for why poor kids did not succeed as adults. Entrenched racism in the labor market, and in the educational and criminal justice systems, was discounted. Beliefs about the poor work habits of black men fueled discrimination against them, and stereotypes about the irresponsibility of black women hastened the end of welfare. Although the majority of welfare recipients had not been black, and most poor people in the United States are white, the images of these conditions were, and continue to be, heavily racialized.

Is it really arguable that two-parent families work better for raising children than do single mothers? Extra adult supervision, labor, and income surely offer the best way to handle the many challenges of parenthood. Same sex couples offer the same advantages, and the growing acceptance of legal marriage between same sex partners, something Moynihan surely did not foresee, complicates the issue from a "traditional" family perspective. Other types of partnerships and arrangements for stable shared responsibility for children in a household can be equally justified in terms of bridging the resource and nurturing gaps associated with single parenthood. Anthropology has taught us that kinship is variable and that functioning families can be shaped in many different ways.

What ultimately seems obvious in the struggling families of poor adults, whether there are one or two parents in a household, is that having financial resources to meet basic needs is the main challenge. Not being able to cobble together a sufficient income causes hardship, stress, and often abuse and neglect. In low-income neighborhoods, especially those inhabited by African Americans and Latinos, the cost of poverty is especially high. The criminalization and incarceration of such a disproportionate share of young men bleeds families of funds, inflicts heartaches on parents and other kin, and reduces the likelihood of marriage for young women.

A large share of the resources devoted to fighting poverty are directed at correcting or punishing misbehaviors of poor people that are thought to be the cause of their problems. Marriage promotion programs are one example. Parenting and "life skills" workshops are another. To the extent that poverty reflects individual failings, policies to reduce poverty should offer services and programs that retrain or rehabilitate people lacking the needed qualities. For those who need personal guidance, retraining, or therapy, such help may be valuable and necessary. However, when plants close or recession strikes, such efforts have little to offer those who are affected. More generally, when employers refuse to hire black workers, and teachers are encouraged to resent and fear black male students, and police repeatedly arrest neighborhood youth for trivial offenses, and predatory lenders and vendors are the only businesses around, then workshops in developing life skills or promoting marriage are not going to be much help.

The tangle of pathology idea, cornerstone of much contemporary poverty policy, directs policy makers to view the problem as individualized. Neoliberal programs that emphasize taking personal responsibility and exiting "bad" neighborhoods are designed along these lines. They often include elements of tough love and unbreakable compacts to instill the discipline that is thought to be lacking. Data-driven social engineering programs attempt to combat poverty by attacking its correlates, like promoting marriage, or mass relocations from neighborhoods of concentrated poverty, or the use of arrest data to find "hot spots" for extra aggressive policing. Practically speaking, these designs often create social dynamics that are counterproductive and unfriendly. Patronizing or punitive treatment flows from the idea that beneficiaries of services are deficient and possibly depraved. Rhetoric, behavior, and the nature of the services themselves may create unspoken hostility or feelings of humiliation. Collaboration and cooperation are made difficult under such conditions, and to the extent that compliance is needed for a program to work, such tensions reduce that likelihood. If the theoretical understanding of a problem is wrong, then the remedies that derive from the theory are likely to be ineffective and even counterproductive. The belief that poverty is caused by an unfolding scenario of pathological values and behavior nurtured in the rough housing and mean streets of inner-city ghettos inverts the process and, as William Ryan said almost half a century ago, blames the victims.

People and Policies

The next three chapters illustrate the consequences of racial stereotypes and tangle of pathology thinking. The issues addressed are housing, criminal justice, and antipoverty programs. Housing and residential segregation have been eternal problems for African Americans. Institutionalized discrimination by lenders and realtors, justified by racist beliefs about housing and neighborhood values, gave birth to a dual housing market that narrowed choices and exacted added costs for substandard housing. The rise and fall of public housing, and the convoluted logic behind the HOPE VI program that demolished much of it, are examined in chapter 4. The scope and impact of mass incarceration on deepening impoverishment and declining marriage in African American communities is the object of chapter 5. Fears of black rage and a long history of black criminalization are examined in the larger context of criminal behavior and damage to the social order. The distorted quality of much rhetoric about race and crime is traced in the paradox of convict leasing in the early to mid-twentieth century, when innocent black men were arrested by sworn public officials and forced to labor at enterprises owned by rich white men who were engaged in mass kidnapping for their personal profit. The owners went unpunished and the victims were tarred with the label of criminals. Private prisons are modern versions of this practice and are among the factors driving up an incarceration rate that has made the United States the undisputed top jailer in the world. The intersection of race, poverty, and incarceration are brought into focus, including the guilt and impunity of an increasingly oligarchic society. The final chapter in this section (chapter 6) looks at the poverty program industry, and the perverse fortunes that have been made by consultants who espouse a culture of poverty message. The growth of poverty in the age of entrepreneurship opened a niche for motivational speakers and purveyors of alleged wisdom about underclass failings. Staff and professional development training and workshops for mentors are designed to aid in cross-class understanding, but often aggravate the conditions described above. Among the most successful are programs that affirm commonly held stereotypes about poor people of various ethnic groups. Ruby Payne's "aha, Inc." offers a prominent example. Payne's workshops, books, and lectures tell teachers, social workers, nonprofit staff and board members, and others involved with poor families or children that poverty is caused by bad parenting and desperate neighborhood environments. The children are presented as innocent up to a certain age, but damaged early by their home environments. Her interpretation resonates with her mostly white middle- and upper middle-class audiences who draw reassurance from the message. "Aha" betokens the comforting awareness that what one suspects is true indeed. Such false reinforcement makes things worse. It encourages condescending and fearful interactions with students and clients that impede cooperation, and then blames failure of programs on the intended beneficiaries, adding more evidence of their personal defects.

In all three chapters I make extended reference to work that my colleagues and I have done in Tampa, Florida over the past thirty years. These excursions are designed to offer grounded examples and lessons from the field about the relatively abstract and sometimes abstruse issues that are raised in discussions of poverty, race, and culture.

4

There Goes the Neighborhood

• • • • • • • • • • • • • • • • •

Deconcentration and
Destruction of
Public Housing

> There is no family structure. They sleep around
> and all that kind of thing. That's the problem
> for the decade, as I see it. We have to break up
> that concentration, get those people out into
> society somehow. I'm about at the point where
> I think they ought to be all stuck in boxcars
> and sent out around, one family to each town.
> —John Ehrlichman

The above words were spoken about African Americans to President Nixon at Camp David in August 1972.[1] Words like "box cars" and "concentration," uttered by a disgraced official in the disgraced administration of Richard Nixon, call up ominous images of forced deportations that are perhaps unsurprising given the source. What may come as a surprise, however, is that the Democratic president, Bill Clinton, embraced Ehrlichman's advice about breaking up what were regarded as pathological concentrations of poor people and scattering them "out into society," presumably for their own good. The policy is known as "deconcentration" and the program designed to enact it (HOPE VI) enabled the destruction of a very large share of public housing in cities throughout the country, a process that has continued under different labels during the Obama administration.[2] If present trends continue, it is foreseeable that all traditional public housing projects could be demolished in the next few years.

Public housing in the United States has been a potent symbol of the assumed pathologies of black poverty. Originating in the Great Depression of the 1930s, pressure on the government to ease the housing crisis arose as much out of concern for reviving the lagging construction industry as for helping citizens attain decent places to live. It was a controversial program that needed to avoid confronting racial segregation and anxieties about public competition with the private housing industry. The contradictions of its origins grew over time into what is deemed an unholy compromise for very low-income families. Images in the media portray snake pit existence and gang rule. Social life within these places has been much more nuanced, but almost no one who does not live there knows about that.[3] Motorists generally cut a wide swath around areas containing public housing projects. Social workers and police arrive to witness and resolve the worst kinds of behavior. Reporters come in when there is crime to be revealed. Readers of newspapers know only about those incidents and understandably generalize to the whole population. Those who do observe the buildings see blight and disrepair, conditions attributed to the inhabitants. Stigma is too mild a word to convey the implied shame visited on these places. The "tangle of pathology" meme is deeply ingrained in views about the inhabitants of public housing in the United States. As explanation and description, public housing has put a face on the problem of urban poverty; largely it is a black face. The damaging perceptual connection between race and poverty, a linkage strongly reinforced by Moynihan's report, is most clearly articulated in stereotypes about people living in public housing.

Often poorly constructed at the outset, structures deteriorated under regimes of diminishing maintenance. In the 1980s the Reagan administration drastically cut funding and operated under rules guaranteed to hasten their decay. Only the poorest families were able to qualify, many of whom could pay no rent at all, and maintenance budgets were to be drawn from rental revenue—a very slim purse to address increasingly challenging problems. A legacy of poor management and corrupt contracting detracted greatly from the adequacy of the housing. By the early 1990s conditions in many complexes had become unlivable, and the upsurge of drug and gang violence of the preceding decade added justification for declaring a crisis. The proposed solution was a program initiated in 1992 known by the anodyne and virtually meaningless acronym, HOPE VI (Housing Opportunities for People Everywhere, part six). Setting aside a long-standing requirement that demolishing units of public housing required one-for-one replacement, HOPE VI funded demolition of distressed complexes that would be replaced by lower density new complexes designed for "mixed income" residents, with only a small share reserved for those poor enough to qualify for public housing. The vast majority of former tenants were simply relocated, using vouchers for private rentals or placement into other still standing public housing complexes. In effect, the new public housing was upgraded, downsized, and made more exclusive; private housing was subsidized for most who were displaced. By the end of the program in 2010, some 255,000 units had been demolished, affecting upwards of half a million people, at a reported cost of $6.2 billion.[4]

The theoretical basis for HOPE VI derived mainly from the work of William Julius Wilson, one of Moynihan's most ardent and consistent admirers. Wilson's 1987 monograph, *The Truly Disadvantaged*, was a self-described attempt to merge structural and cultural explanations of inner-city black poverty.[5] The introduction is replete with praise for Moynihan and frustration with what Wilson described as the intimidation of cultural inquiry brought about by radical opposition to *The Negro Family*. Labeling denizens of inner-city black neighborhoods as the "urban underclass," Wilson proceeded to craft an explanation for their enduring and deepening poverty. Two factors were implicated. First was deindustrialization, which removed opportunities for employment from these areas. Second was the departure of middle- and upper-class African Americans who had been able to relocate into previously closed neighborhoods outside of the ghetto due to the gains of the Civil Rights movement. Their leaving removed what Wilson regarded as critical role models and potential ladders to mobility, delivering these zones to the negative cultural influences of those left behind, "increasingly isolated socially from mainstream patterns of norms and behavior."[6] This combination of suppressed economic opportunities and unfettered cultural pathology had, in Wilson's view, created the abject conditions of inner cities in the 1980s. His focus was on the debilitating effects of "concentrated poverty," wherein youth and otherwise competent adults were trapped in a self-defeating social system. Isolation was the problem, caused by both reduced employment opportunities and an absence of positive social influences. Zones of concentrated poverty were declared to be festering with bad behavior and dysfunctional examples, a contagious infection of the civic body. Public housing epitomized this presumed sociocultural affliction.

Wilson, a respected black sociologist then at the University of Chicago, drew substantial support for this line of thinking in the increasingly neoliberal policy environment of the 1980s and '90s. By focusing also on systemic shifts in the geography of work, he countered the unalloyed racism of popular writers like Charles Murray who attributed black poverty solely to the tangle of pathology identified by Moynihan (and reinforced by what Murray regarded as a wrong-headed welfare policy).[7] Wilson did agree that the culture of underclass neighborhoods played a major role in the perpetuation of dysfunctional behavior. Although he grounded his argument in the structural shifts that greatly reduced and relocated manufacturing jobs, his exposition emphasized most heavily the behavioral consequences for individuals and what he described as an insidiously broad cultural impact for the whole group left stranded in these zones. Like Moynihan, Wilson decried the rise in female-headed households, although he discounted historical causes rooted in slavery. He was mainly concerned with cultural explanations for contemporary problems, combining an emphasis on failing families within a dystopic environment that created and reinforced bad behavior and negative influences. The focus on concentration effects drew high-level attention to Wilson's work and powerfully shaped ideas about urban policy.

If concentration posed the immediate problem, then "deconcentration" should offer the most efficient solution. The idea was to eliminate the problems attributed to concentrated poverty by relocating residents of these areas into other parts of the city, suburbs, exurbs, and even rural townships. Relocation was believed to accomplish two goals: move poor people to areas with better schools, less crime and blight, and more employment opportunities; and break up infectious pockets of bad behavior and cultural pathology, exposing individuals (especially youth) to new role models and better social connections. HOPE VI directly implemented this idea in cities throughout the United States. As a test of the concept, HUD funded a quasi-experimental demonstration project in five cities called "Moving to Opportunity" (MTO). The MTO design involved random assignment of public housing residents into three conditions: (1) relocation with a voucher and counseling into census tracts with low poverty (less than 10 percent); (2) relocation with a voucher, but without counseling, to wherever replacement housing might be found; and (3) a control group who simply remained in public housing. The larger program and the experiment ran concurrently, although voucher relocations under HOPE VI mirrored only the second MTO condition, and before it was over a great many in the MTO public housing control group had been displaced by HOPE VI from their public housing complexes. Extended naturalistic experiments on people leading their everyday lives are difficult to conduct. History and politics frequently intervene, and in this instance there was a near total collapse of the housing market in 2007–2008.

HUD invested more than $6 billion in HOPE VI between 1992 and 2011 (about $24,000 per unit demolished). Even before the financial crisis, it was having no discernible effect on the actual incidence of poverty. It just spread poor folks around. Results of the MTO evaluation and a multi-year, multi-site panel study of HOPE VI by the Urban Institute (in Atlantic City, Chicago, Durham, Richmond, and Washington, DC, in 2001, 2003, and 2005) were disappointing at best. Among those who were relocated, there was no measurable improvement in either employment or school achievement. Health status among HOPE VI relocatees actually declined in comparison with those still living in public housing.[8] And an increased number of male youth were involved with criminal justice. A recent study of 1,407 MTO boys who were less than eight years old when they moved, and were followed eleven years later, found they had significantly higher levels of depression, PTSD, and conduct disorder than boys in the control group who had remained in public housing.[9] These were not young "thugs" who moved into a new neighborhood, but small children who grew up in places where neighbors, school experiences, and police nurtured alienation and acute psychological distress. The only positive results of HOPE VI have been self-reports of greater housing satisfaction and perceived reductions in disorder, and relatively better psychological results for MTO females (as indicated by Kessler et al. in the study cited above).

Between 2000 and 2007 I was principal investigator on a series of grants that funded research about relocations out of two large public housing complexes in Tampa, Florida. The study involved initial interviews with a cross section of relocated residents very shortly after they had moved in 2000. Three years later, with a grant from the National Science Foundation, we interviewed randomly selected HOPE VI relocatees and homeowners in two destination neighborhoods with respectively low and high poverty rates. We did a follow-up project in 2007 in the mixed income complex that was built on the site of one of the demolished projects, and we conducted interviews with new homeowners in single-family homes that had been constructed on the other one. Also in 2005–2007 we participated in a prolonged collaboration with the Tampa Housing Authority, which was then planning to demolish another large public housing complex. These interconnected research projects offered a long, intense, and varied perspective on how the HOPE VI program worked in one city. During the same period in cities throughout the United States other researchers were engaged in similar assessments.[10]

There are two basic issues. First, how did relocated families fare in the private neighborhoods with vouchers that enabled (but did not require) them to live where average incomes were higher and housing was better? Second, what were the outcomes in the new mixed income complexes designed to engineer inter class social contact and positive role models for low-income households? In both cases the goal was to free impoverished families from the toxic effects of concentrated poverty. This was a multibillion dollar effort based on the belief that poverty is both caused and aggravated by the dense proximity of poor people to each other, and that simply dispersing them would yield both social and economic improvements. As indicated above, evaluations suggest that it did not work out that way on the ground, but what causal dynamics were revealed in examinations of this process across time and a wide span of urban geography? Before examining those questions in greater detail, however, let's consider the larger context.

Antecedents and Impediments

Deconcentration was a bold experiment in social engineering designed to combat residential segregation by race and class that for more than a century has been ingrained in real estate, lending, public policy, and widely accepted notions regarded as common sense. Moving large numbers of very poor, mostly black residents out of public housing and into private neighborhoods was a radical approach. Developing new attractive apartment complexes on the sullied sites of some of the nation's most notorious public housing projects was similarly daring. Would incumbent residents of existing neighborhoods be willing to accept and mentor an influx of poorer residents drawn from the dangerous underclass? Would middle-class families be attracted to new apartments in what had been regarded as dangerous neighborhoods? Multiple layers of resistance could have been predicted. Neighborhoods are where people keep their belongings, children, and other defenseless family members. Fears of crime and bad influences on kids are not minor concerns in choosing a neighborhood, or deciding to stay in one. Associations among blackness, poverty, and crime are extremely prevalent and backed up by highly disparate statistics on arrests, sentencing, and incarceration. In the next chapter, we will examine these relationships more closely, but as a widespread belief in American society, the strength of the connection between these beliefs cannot be denied.

Real estate values are an added source of worry. Since the early years of the twentieth century both banking and insurance practices have explicitly discounted the value of property located in all-black or mixed neighborhoods. The FHA formalized these criteria in 1938 with the adoption of maps that literally "redlined" such neighborhoods as places considered too risky for lending. Private legally binding covenants protected white owners from the possibility that houses in their vicinity might be sold to African Americans by preventing individual owners from selling to such buyers. Although the Supreme Court struck down racial covenants in 1948 (*Shelley v. Kraemer*), it was not until the Fair Housing Act of 1968 that discrimination in housing was actually forbidden by law. And even then institutional and informal discrimination persisted. Real estate analysts like Anthony Downs of the Brookings Institution constructed models of housing value and neighborhood decline that assigned black residents, irrespective of income, as a negative variable.[11] This categorization was inherently discriminatory against black owners or sellers, and yielded a self-fulfilling prophecy of neighborhood decline. Urban renewal programs of the 1960s and '70s, which also displaced large numbers of poor black households, unleashed a vicious real estate scheme called "block busting" in which short-term profits were gleaned by arousing terrifying prospects among settled homeowners in older urban neighborhoods, precipitating what came to be known as white flight. Those neighborhoods were hence battered by excessive vacancies and the inability of owners to obtain loans for maintenance. Given that history and similar ongoing practices, contemporary worries about possible loss of housing value from changes in racial composition of one's neighborhood are entirely rational.

Potential effects of fear of crime or diminished housing values in relocation sites are not mentioned in the literature that promotes deconcentration as a policy. The alleged benefits of mixed income housing originate mainly from writing about the New Urbanism, chiefly an architectural movement that pays homage to aesthetic and utopian visions of urban space, neglecting the history of real estate greed and interracial strife.[12] HOPE IV began late in the Bush I administration, was enthusiastically expanded by Clinton, and further promoted by Bush II. Liberal social scientists who admirably condemned the wretched record of unequal housing and segregated neighborhoods in the United States have found much to like in a policy designed to promote racial integration and better housing and neighborhoods for families who have been prevented from accessing them. Privatization using vouchers and public/private partnerships in redevelopment, combined with a huge reduction in public housing units, appealed to conservatives. Local elected officials were especially grateful for the opportunity to clear blighted zones in central city areas that were being revitalized as crime rates fell and young professionals were returning to urban lifestyles. Some politicians appreciated the fact that dense blocs of black voters were being broken up and scattered into other areas. Given the varied benefits to such a wide array of powerful sectors, possible problems both for those who were moved and their prospective new neighbors were conveniently ignored.

Backlash

As might have been predicted, however, relocations have brought forth a lot of angry resistance by incumbents, who rarely have been willing to serve as mentors and role models for former residents of public housing. In Tampa we interviewed a sizable sample of homeowners in the two neighborhoods we studied. By a wide margin they were unhappy with the program and not on board with their presumed role in making it work. They did not want to be part of some social engineering scheme that placed what they considered to be pathological families into their midst, endangering their children and harming their property values. The size and quality of social networks pre- and post-relocation decreased greatly for both incumbents and relocatees. Role models were scarce, but aggressive policing was prevalent, yielding increased youth involvement with criminal justice instead of new avenues to success. In our low-poverty neighborhood, vigilante behavior by some homeowners was aimed at securing evictions of those new families who could be detected doing anything wrong. In one mixed income redevelopment composed of rental apartments and owner-occupied single-family homes, the home-owners' association mobilized against the renters, calling on our research team at one point to help mediate the struggle. This occurred in spite of severe eligibility criteria for determining which former public housing tenants would be allowed to return, and strict rules about public behavior for those who moved in. Fear more than reality inspired these aversions and frictions.

Results similar to ours have been reported in many other cities (e.g., Chicago, Atlanta, Baltimore, Philadelphia, and Washington, DC). In Baltimore the MTO program was nearly shut down because of organized opposition from incumbent neighbors in low-poverty areas.[13] A study in one of Atlanta's HOPE VI redevelopment projects also discovered very unhappy owners. On one side of the street was a mixed income apartment complex composed of renters, including former public housing residents. On the other side was a small subdivision of owner-occupied single-family houses that had been built with federal money and offered mortgage subsidies for new owners. Virtually all the owners were black and middle-class.[14] Their presence effectively reproduced Wilson's vertically integrated pre–Civil Rights African American neighborhood of yore, where intact families of higher classes lived close and reportedly could offer mentoring and positive examples for those who were poor. To the extent that this new development reflects Wilson's counterfactual vision, it has proved highly disconfirming. Similar to the Tampa example cited above, the Atlanta homeowners worried excessively about the presence and behavior of the renters and avoided contact with them to the extent possible. Their concerns were not matched by actual incidents of crime or violence, but rather spurred by their beliefs about the dangerousness of the people who lived too close by. Such aversions are not new. St. Clair Drake and Horace Cayton's classic study of Bronzeville, Chicago's sprawling historically African American district, revealed numerous examples of disdain and avoidance by upper income residents of their low-income neighbors in the 1930s and '40s. Du Bois also describes avoidant distinctions in Philadelphia's black neighborhoods in the late nineteenth century, and Gregory reports similar social dynamics in the late twentieth-century neighborhood of Elmhurst-Corona in New York.[15] It seems that the lost historical inter-class social compact that Wilson invoked to counsel deconcentration may actually never have been in force.

Wilson coedited a book (with Richard Taub) in 2006 titled *There Goes the Neighborhood* that showed clearly what kind of resistance could have been expected.[16] Based on a study of four Chicago working-class neighborhoods (white, black, and Latino), it revealed a large degree of determined resistance to incursions of darker and/or poorer residents in all of these areas. Despite these findings, and a final chapter on policy implications, the authors drew no connection to deconcentration or HOPE VI. Although they expressed optimism that this resistance could be transitory, a century of neighborhood research by University of Chicago sociologists, inventors of the "invasion-succession" hypothesis, has shown this same pattern generation after generation. Given a mountain of contrary evidence, it seems disingenuous to have theorized smooth integration and improvements in social capital for newly arrived poor families within such freighted contexts.

The social purposes of deconcentration clearly have not worked out as planned. Few role models or mentors have materialized; aversion and antipathy reign instead. Much of the reflexive resistance can be credited to the stigma that public housing residents carry, which this program does nothing to combat—quite the opposite. Such reactions are baked into the deconcentration formula. If the main rationale for relocation is that public housing tenants exert bad influences on each other and hence need to be dispersed, then it should not be surprising that these alleged social characteristics would be unwelcome in the sites where they landed. The tangle of pathology meme, which Moynihan made famous and Wilson happily adopted, is itself a self-perpetuating and self-fulfilling idea. Prejudgment and stereotyping doomed this experiment in social mixing, and built on concerns of parents and homeowners that were too fundamental to set aside in the name of casual hospitality.

Costs of Relocation

Newly arrived HOPE VI relocatees have not been welcomed warmly and shown the path to more successful lives by their more successful neighbors. But aren't they still better off to be out of the projects and inserted into more mainstream lives? Actually, only a bare majority of those who have gone into private housing are living in what they describe as better housing. Most HOPE VI and MTO participants ultimately moved into neighborhoods not appreciably different from the ones they left, and in many cases their new arrangements have proved to be far less affordable.[17] A large share, up to one-half in many cities and about one-third in Tampa, were simply placed into other public housing projects little better than the ones that were torn down. Often these new placements were temporary, waiting for the HOPE VI project that would uproot them once again, and maybe yet another time when the next complex was demolished. Those with vouchers also showed a pattern of instability. Many who had spent years in the same apartment in public housing found that, for various reasons, they were required to move frequently in their new status of voucher holders.[18] Very few were able to return to the redeveloped mixed income complexes built on the sites they had left. Rules for entry were stiff, allowing no background problems and no history of troublemaking. In the mixed income redevelopment in Tampa that we studied, virtually all of the former public housing residents were elderly women; less than 7 percent of the households who had been displaced made it into the new complex.[19] It is noteworthy that the former public housing residents in the new complex occupied relatively less desirable units, and they were treated disrespectfully by the private management company. Although it was supposed to be a socially integrated development, the public housing stigma remained in the mental taxonomy of the management, and to a lesser extent among the market rate tenants.

HOPE VI was an involuntary program, and the residents of complexes slated for demolition had virtually no part in deciding whether or how that process would go forward. They all had to leave. For some who had long hoped to escape into private housing but had no chance of ever getting a voucher before, the program was a godsend. They gladly began the process of searching for a new neighborhood. The move was hard on many families, however, especially elderly tenants who had lived in their homes a long time. Two older sisters who had lived next door to each other in a Tampa project were moved to apartments that were miles apart. They spoke on the phone each day, but rarely were able to see each other and grieved for the company that they had given each other. It was hard on young mothers with low-paid jobs and no cars. Scarce and costly day care and inadequate bus transportation in new places posed serious challenges that sometimes caused them to lose their jobs. It was hard on a lot of teens thrust into strange neighborhoods where established cliques and gangs made their lives miserable and worse. Relocation was presented as a way to save youth and give them a better chance, but moving is a major risk factor for school failure in low-income children, and the adult neighbors who used to know and often help them were replaced with strangers who feared them and too often reacted with loathing and threats.[20] Policing in these areas has been especially intense, and kids are often arrested for minor or contrived offenses. Such treatment bears a heavy cost, and many of the young men we got to know in one of the relocation neighborhoods have ended up in prison. Relocation was also hard on eighteen-year-olds from large families, who were often forced to move on their own with vouchers, because large apartments that could hold all the children in large families were in short supply. One young woman we learned about in our study was sexually assaulted by an intruder shortly after moving reluctantly to an apartment of her own. Grandmothers raising children were often separated from them due to the need to relocate into senior housing, where kids are not allowed. Friends and kin accustomed to living close to each other had great difficulty re-creating those conditions in the relocation.

By design, the program impeded or ruptured existing social ties that were in many cases both instrumental and emotional. Survival in the projects was for many based on an exchange of services that were critical to ensure the safety of children, hold a job, obtain transport to the doctor, use a telephone, and enjoy the small favors and pleasant encounters that humanize social relations among neighbors. Distanced analyses of life in the projects have overlooked these elements. In contrast, ethnographies in housing projects challenge the uniformly awful images that are portrayed in media and reflected in census and crime statistics. Close-up inspections of how life has been lived in these places reveal intricate underground economies that do include drugs and stolen goods, but also a vast array of informal services and protective arrangements that mitigate painfully low incomes and dangers posed by drugs, gangs, and corrupt police.[21] Instances of pathological behavior do occur in the form of violence, physical abuse, and neglect. But so do organized kindness, mutual surveillance, and highly creative ways of helping oneself and others. In most of the projects in Tampa, some older women assumed the role of "grandma" to all the kids in the neighborhood, walking them to and from school, letting them stay in their units until mothers returned from work, helping in various ways to ensure safety and provide affection. Although some relationships between neighbors were disputatious and even violent, mutual aid and neighborly sociality was more common, as were norms of helping those with sudden calamities. In Tampa one of the families who was relocated arrived at their new apartment and awaited the truck containing all of their belongings (which had been contracted by the Housing Authority). It never came. The drivers apparently took it elsewhere, stripped everything of value and disposed of the rest. All their furniture and household goods disappeared and they were left with nothing in an empty apartment. Fortunately they were in a large complex that contained more than a dozen other HOPE VI families they knew from the projects. These other relocatees mobilized among themselves enough spare furnishings to enable this family to sleep on beds and cook their food.

Breaking up the social ties of public housing residents was an unbidden favor that HOPE VI presumed to offer, one of the singular benefits that the program advocates claimed would occur. In place of these allegedly dysfunctional relationships, they believed new, more valuable connections could be nurtured through proximal contact with a better class of neighbors. As indicated earlier, that part of the formula failed to materialize. Untangling the social networks of public housing residents was also a wrongheaded and cruel idea based on assumptions that might have been disabused with a more qualitative and collaborative approach to the research on which they were based. So strong was the conviction that their "culture" was causing their problems, that the pathology was endogenous to the social influences among families who lived there, that they were subjected to a social experiment that actually caused more damage. Instead of the presumed cultural deficiencies of the former tenants, an alternative explanation for their impoverished and unhappy condition might be sought by examining the institutional circumstances that negatively affected their ability to succeed and created an undesirable environment for both children and adults.

Externalities

The quality of the housing and physical environment in public housing projects is typically awful. By original agreement with the real estate industry, public housing was deliberately constructed to be inferior to what was available in the private market. Amenities that are taken for granted were generally lacking. For example, in Tampa some complexes were built without closet doors, with the rationale that this feature would coerce the residents into keeping the contents neat. Stinginess combined with corruption produced original construction that cut corners and yielded substandard results—walls too thin to keep out noise, windows too ill-fitting to keep out insects and cold, and plumbing prone to leaks and the growth of mold—conditions that worsened over time. Serious gaps in maintenance began with the drastic budget cuts of the 1980s that were never restored. Worse than these problems was the ubiquity of lead paint, a huge health risk known to cause severe neurological damage. The dangers of lead exposure were known for decades before it was finally banned in 1978. Although lead paint was eliminated from new construction and abated in much of the older private housing, until quite recently HUD refused to act to reduce the risk in the hundreds of thousands of units it oversaw. Besides living with roaches, mold, and other risky contaminants, children growing up in public housing have extremely high levels of asthma, lead poisoning, and other conditions that affect their ability to do well in school or maintain good health.

It is important to point out that the above conditions are not caused by the behavioral pathology of residents. To the contrary, these conditions cause serious medical pathology, the real kind that stunts and shortens lives. And the blight observed by those passing by the projects does not reflect the careless behavior of the tenants. It is not their responsibility to clear trash or paint the buildings. In most cases they are not allowed to plant flowers or decorate their exteriors. More significantly, they don't control the contaminants that make their children sick. A woman we interviewed in Tampa had called the Health Department to report what she was certain was lead paint in her apartment and also the human waste that oozed from a broken sewer connection in her backyard. After her daughter tested positive for lead poisoning, the Health Department forced the Housing Authority to relocate them to another unit in a different complex. They put the family in a project that was older than the one they had been living in, and where a half dozen children in the vicinity also tested positive for lead poisoning only a few months after the family moved in. This came as no surprise, but was utterly disheartening because the daughter was already showing symptoms of the poisoning in her behavior at school. The woman was worried about her younger child in this new environment but was helpless. When she initially had been told where they would be moved, her well-founded fears were rebuffed: "I asked that lady [at the Housing Authority], I said, 'all these projects have been built around the same time. I know every last one of these projects got lead poison in them.' [But] she said 'no.' And I can't argue with them cause I ain't got nowhere to go."

It would at least be progress if HOPE VI removed families from this kind of threat. However, many of the units in Tampa where they were relocated were also constructed before 1978, and the inspectors refused to check for lead before granting landlords voucher approval. The director of the Health Department had devised a simple checklist for them to use, but they claimed it would add to their work and suggested that if she was worried about it, she could do the inspections herself. At that time, the Housing Authority was faced with the task of relocating 1,200 families, and possibly they did not want to disqualify potential places where they could put them.

Management Pathology

Housing Authorities nationwide offer well-known examples of bad management and authoritarian leadership. Certainly not all, but a great many treat residents with disrespect, suppress their efforts to participate in decisions that vitally affect them, capriciously enforce draconian eviction policies ("one strike and you are out"), and do a poor job of responding to legitimate problems with disrepair and social control. The Chicago Housing Authority is a well-known example. Sudhir Venkatesh's monograph about the Robert Taylor Homes recounts numerous negligent and corrupt practices and incidents of maltreatment of residents. Alex Kotlowitz's book about Henry Horner Homes, also in Chicago, includes similar accounts.[22] A Google search using the keywords "corrupt Housing Authority" produces pages of references to stories about abusive and dishonest housing officials from states across the country. The Tampa Housing Authority (THA) was briefly under investigation by HUD, and at this writing remained the subject of a Senate Committee inquiry, for overspending on staff salaries and travel, while withholding needed resources for repairs in the complexes they manage.[23]

In the summer of 2011 I was contacted by a woman who worked in a local agency asking for help with a situation in one of Tampa's housing projects still in existence (but since slated for demolition). THA had issued hundreds of official notices to tenants, nearly all the families in the complex, demanding that they pay for costly repairs to their air conditioners, due within seven days, or they would face eviction. The problem began with improper work by THA staff who installed window units that left a large gap permitting insects, hot air, and in some cases intruders to enter apartments. Tenants had improvised their own repairs for this unlivable problem, which were suddenly being cited as lease violations. To fix the problem, THA was seeking $110 to reinstall each window unit, under threat of tenants' losing their housing. Some apartments had as many as four units. This constituted an enormous sum for families whose incomes were among the lowest in the city. Although these conditions had existed for a long time, and the property manager in charge of the faulty work had been fired months earlier, there was a forced urgency in the response demanded. An upcoming HUD inspection seemed to be the impetus for this action, and the tenants were being required to pay the cost of rectifying the problem.

The tenant association responded with a protest meeting, and a reporter for a local newspaper attended. The US representative whose district includes the complex formally demanded an explanation. Under pressure THA agreed to work out long-term payment plans, but did not dismiss the charges. In the weeks and months that followed, the tenant who organized the meeting encountered a crescendo of complaints and provocations from the management of the complex and higher level staff. After a series of legal skirmishes that resulted in a written agreement that he signed under duress without legal representation, they obtained a default judgment in court without his knowledge that evicted him and his family of five young children he was raising alone, with only twenty-four hours' notice. The record of an eviction made it extremely difficult to find another apartment and disqualified him from receiving financial assistance for the move. What appeared to be retaliation for exercising his rights as an officer of the tenant association and affected resident of the complex proved costly for him and his family, and served as an example for anyone else who would dare to do the same. During the same period that THA was attempting to cadge scarce dollars from extremely poor people, they were accused of having spent lavishly on a new headquarters for themselves, located in an upscale district several miles from any of the complexes they manage, and paying the director a salary that exceeded by half the amount legally allowed by HUD.[24] Staff reportedly took expensive trips to conferences and workshops in enticing locales, where they possibly received training in how best to manage their "pathological tenants." This incident is not an isolated example; the previous director of THA had been convicted of criminal corruption and sentenced to a long prison term (from which he was eventually granted relief). The current management, even with all its bullying, is regarded as a big improvement, and the director has enjoyed an extremely long tenure.

The evicted activist was no firebrand. Despite a seriously disabling condition and five children he was raising by himself, he had been a reliable volunteer in his complex, organizing the Crime Watch, holiday food distributions, and after-school tutoring. In addition to his office in the tenant association, he was active in the PTA in the nearby elementary school. He was taking courses at the local community college to earn a counseling degree and hopefully provide a better future for his children. These praiseworthy activities were insufficient to shield him from the wrath of the authorities he dared to question. He is perhaps atypical of the many struggling and sometimes failing families who inhabited the housing project where he lived, but their shortcomings pale in comparison to the punishing venality of many who have made and enforced the rules by which the tenants are required to live.

Conditions like those described in the previous pages do cause many families to want to leave the projects. Harsh treatment of tenants tends to be tolerated because stability of residence is considered a bad outcome. The philosophy is that public housing should be a stepping stone, a respite in which families should husband their resources in order to move into the mainstream, rather than be encouraged to stay. However, these same conditions from which rational people want to escape also detract from their ability to do so. From a policy standpoint, such negative incentives should not be encouraged. Any people who are treated this way should have the right to object and be heard. The idea that all who live in public housing, where shelter is truly affordable if not very desirable, should be forced to leave, and that forced relocation is in their best interests, is highly problematic.

Lessons Not Learned

Evaluations of HOPE VI and MTO comprised a naturalistic experiment assessing the premise that bad neighborhoods cause negative social dynamics, which in turn reinforces poverty. The policy of removing poor people from these environments into better neighborhoods, with few added services or interventions against their individual impoverishment, apparently offered a way to determine if poverty could be alleviated by simply changing locales and reordering the ecology of social contact. A generation has passed since the onset of this experiment, and the results do not support original predictions about beneficial change. A bare majority report they are happier with their housing, a response that might be deemed questionable when given to official interviewers who they might fear could jeopardize the vouchers of those who complain. Improved mental health for girls in the experimental condition of MTO constitutes the other positive finding, juxtaposed against significantly higher rates of depression and PTSD among young males. Altogether, not much of a yield from the enormous investment in the MTO project, and the really huge amount that HOPE VI cost taxpayers and a large portion of residents who were forced to move but did not want to do so. Nevertheless, these disappointing outcomes have done little to diminish faith in the original premise. Researchers who invested in the project and staked their careers on making it work have shown a great reluctance to give it up. The search has continued in earnest for evidence that "where you live affects your life chances."[25]

William Julius Wilson's ideas about the ill effects of concentrated poverty and Douglas Massey and Nancy Denton's well-regarded book about urban racial segregation, *American Apartheid* (1993), have inspired a vast amount of quantitative research into what have come to be known as "neighborhood effects."[26] The premise is that the collective social environment of very poor neighborhoods nurtures a congeries of negative behavioral outcomes—drug abuse, delinquency and crime, teen pregnancy, family disorganization, school failures—the tangle of pathology that Moynihan condensed into a single catchphrase connoting all the ills he associated with self-perpetuating poverty. The directionality of this phenomenon is important. The spatial correlations among data on these conditions are not contested. The issue is what causes what. Do poor people simply gravitate to places they can afford, i.e., low-income neighborhoods with cheap rent? Is this an example of the ecological fallacy, wherein agglomeration of distressed individuals in space (neighborhood selection) is mistaken for a syndrome that infects the environment and all who live there?

Poverty is a hard life. A large number of people who are in it engage in behaviors that make things worse, but many others do not. Moreover, conditions like overpolicing, teachers who disrespect their students, and the exploitative behavior of payday lenders, predatory mortgage brokers, and others who capitalize on the vulnerability of poor people, impede their chances to overcome poverty and gain a foothold in the middle class. Substandard schools, a shortage of recreational spaces, and a lack of accessible employment opportunities are also features of this landscape. Ladders to economic mobility and security are objectively lacking even for the virtuous. The alternative belief is that bad behavior is spawned by bad examples and socialization into groups for whom dysfunctional or illegal activity is normative. If Moynihan was right, then the latter is the driving force. The research on neighborhood effects is guided by a conviction that he was.

Based on data drawn from the census, other official records, and large-scale recurring interview projects and panel studies, researchers have searched for causal links between poor neighborhoods and pathological behavior of their residents. They have used increasingly sophisticated statistical techniques in an effort to tease out the individual and areal characteristics that appear to be responsible for stubborn rates of poverty, persistent segregation, and the varied measures of dysfunction that are so closely associated with both conditions. Discovering causal links, however, has been a daunting task, always haunted by objections based on selection, unmeasured variables, and the ecological fallacy. The randomized experimental approach used in MTO was touted as the solution to that problem, but it failed to deliver in terms of both methodology and results.

Robert Sampson, a sociologist who has worked in Chicago's neighborhoods for many years, and whose statistical prowess is widely admired, has dissected MTO in Chicago and discovered that it did not really accomplish what it set out to do. Susan Clampet-Lundquist and Douglas Massey came to the same conclusion. Both articles were published in a 2008 special issue of the *American Journal of Sociology*, "Moving to Opportunity: A Symposium."[27] The vast majority of MTO participants did not move to substantially better neighborhoods, or stay in them long enough to be affected by the hoped-for beneficial treatment. In many cases, youth continued to attend the same schools as they had before moving, and the effects of relocations out of public housing put many who had been in control groups into virtually the same neighborhoods as people in the other two conditions in the experiment. In effect, the treatment was overruled by the volition of the participants and the impact of HOPE VI as it proceeded in parallel with the experiment and altered the control condition.

Sampson contends that MTO also erred by focusing on individual outcomes when a more productive approach would involve focusing on neighborhoods as the units of analysis. His own work has followed that path, coining a concept he calls "collective efficacy" that will be described in greater detail in the final chapter of this book. Sampson does not, however, repudiate Wilson's and Moynihan's ideas about neighborhood effects and tangles of pathology. For example, he argues that lack of improvement through relocation may simply reflect the early impact of life in poor neighborhoods on the cognitive abilities of people who grew up in them. Moving them as adults would not improve their capacity to make productive choices or overcome a kind of Stockholm Syndrome where they are illogically attached to dangerous and negative places. This interpretation suggests a disturbing kind of essentialism that implies permanent damage to the so-called underclass. What policies can be invoked to address that kind of problem? Alternatively, those who refused to comply with a treatment that would take them to unfamiliar and predictably hostile neighborhoods lacking in transportation and far from friends, family, and familiar haunts could have been simply pursuing their own best interests. Engineered relocation as a cure for poverty may be rationally unattractive to people who have a lot more experience with that condition than those who designed the program.

All of this intricate microscopic inspection and analysis of poor people's behavior, associations, attitudes, test scores, residential habits and movements, employability, and family values cannot begin to explain why poverty increased so dramatically over the years since the financial crisis of 2008, from slightly over 11 percent in 2000 to 15 percent in 2010, one of the steepest and most sustained increases in recent history. Was there a sudden outbreak of pathological behavior in the lower middle class that prompted so many to fall into poverty?[28] Perhaps ironically, the mortgage meltdown greatly affected many of the "opportunity neighborhoods" where public housing residents were relocated. One of the neighborhoods in our study became ground zero for foreclosures in Tampa, a city with a notoriously high rate of failed mortgages. Nearly one in four residential structures in the study neighborhood went into foreclosure, and the poverty rate spiked from 43 percent to 52 percent. Sidewalks were frequently littered with the belongings of evicted tenants, many of whom paid their rent on time to landlords who had stopped making mortgage payments. Groveland, the stable black neighborhood in Wilson and Taub's book about resistance to low-income newcomers, has been wracked with foreclosures and was the site of a large amount of predatory lending.[29] Additionally, the austerity that has accompanied the so-called Great Recession has resulted in diminished public services and a tattered safety net. Recreation programs and summer jobs for youth have been severely reduced. Poor people did not cause that, but they have paid dearly for it.

The title of this chapter, "There Goes the Neighborhood," has a dual meaning. On the one hand, it is a cliché for the reactions of white flight and defensive resistance that occur in working-class neighborhoods when visibly poor people move in. HOPE VI, like urban renewal before it, caused upheavals in such neighborhoods, both black and white. The other meaning refers to the loss of community in public housing projects, the literal erasure of spaces that people called home. There has been a strong tendency to deny the existence of positive relationships or valuable social formations within such apparently blighted contexts. Oppositional traditions in social research, reflected in David Harvey's "right to the city" movement, David Imbroscio's critique of what he calls the "dispersal consensus," and Mindy Fullilove's discussion of the problems associated with "root shock," challenge the careless destruction of ties between people that have humanized miserable conditions and spawned collective solutions to shared problems.[30] Small numbers of unwanted refugees in hostile neighborhoods are arguably more "socially isolated" than multi-generational communities who share poverty but also each other. Rather than addressing directly the many problems of the environment in which they lived, applying funds to improvements, and dealing with management problems and corruption, the decision was made to spend the money on demolition and the creation of new complexes that few of the former residents were able to inhabit.

The effort to destroy public housing projects has largely succeeded. In Atlanta all the former complexes have been demolished. In other cities, including Tampa, some still stand but future demolition seems certain. Without HOPE VI, other mechanisms have been found, including the Obama administration's replacement programs called Choice Neighborhoods and Neighborhoods of Promise, and improvised public-private partnerships that permit demolition of public housing as part of larger redevelopment projects.[31] The supply of low-income housing, especially for those who are "truly disadvantaged," has shrunk and rents in most cities have increased. Waiting lists of those seeking vouchers are years long, and these subsidies are a fragile benefit easily cut by a Congress unsympathetic to expenditures on the poor. The rationale that poor people have wrought their own misery, or that private charity can better sort the deserving from the rest, joins a growing chorus of reasons for the reductions in aid.

Inequality of income and wealth is greater than it has been in the past hundred years, since it first was measured.[32] There also has been a rising inequality in the criminal justice system. The biggest perpetrators of fraudulent mortgage deals and other financial misdeeds, the cause of the crisis that plunged the economy into recession, have not been punished, whereas the incarceration rate for nonviolent drug offenders has soared. The next chapter will examine the issue of crime in the tangle of pathology, looking also at the top of the income pyramid where bad decisions, amorality, and fraudulent acts have had arguably much greater consequences than the street crime of poor people and their neighborhoods.

5

Crime, Criminals, and
Tangles of Pathology

• • • • • • • • • • • • • • • • • •

> This is where the new despotism is hidden,
> in these thousands of arbitrary decisions that
> surround our otherwise transparent system
> of real jury trials and carefully enumerated
> suspects' rights. This vast extrademocratic
> mechanism, it turns out, is made up of injus-
> tices big and small, from sweeping national
> concepts like Eric Holder's Collateral Con-
> sequences plan granting situational leniency
> to "systemically important" companies, to
> smaller more localized outrages like New
> York City prosecutors subverting speedy trial
> rules in order to extract guilty pleas from poor
> defendants who can't make bail.
> —Matt Taibbi, *The Great Divide*

What is social pathology? In particular, what is the connection between poverty and crime? Or between wealth and crime? Are African Americans more prone to commit crimes than members of other groups? Are rich people more likely to be psychopaths than those with little money? A brief deconstruction of the concepts of crime and pathology could look like this: Who is a worse threat to the social order—a single mother on food stamps who works off the books caring for her neighbors' children, her teenage son who sells marijuana on the corner, or a Wall Street banker who steals people's houses and loots municipal pension funds? Most people would say the Wall Street guy has done the worst harm. The US judicial system chooses the kid and then his mother, and rarely does much of anything to punish financial criminals.

In this chapter I'll examine the importance of race and class in the operation of the criminal justice system, highlight deeply rooted racial disparities, and also consider the extent to which a disproportionate number of upstanding wealthy citizens exhibit social pathologies more generally attributed to poor people. Finally, recent analyses by economists that connect the rise in poverty directly with the growing inequality of wealth will be contrasted with theories about the causes of poverty that follow the logic of the Moynihan Report.

Crime and delinquency formed a conspicuous element in Moynihan's model of tangled pathology arising from female-headed households. When the report was released, rising crime rates and perceived disorder were already spurring a right-wing backlash. The coincidental Watts uprising in the summer of 1965 pumped oxygen into news stories about the report. Robert Novak's column made specific reference to the lessons it held for understanding the outbreak of violence, and directly quoted Moynihan's statement that earlier urban riots had prompted him to research and write it. Street crime, protest, and spontaneous outbursts of anger were becoming conflated. The subtext was that African Americans were dangerous, that poverty combined with inept upbringing and untamed rage were all coming to the surface in the successes of the Civil Rights movement. The electoral value of these fears helped put Richard Nixon in the White House and promoted a war on drugs that would dramatically alter the criminal justice system and create literally millions of second-class citizens.

Strangely, while the drug war was driving up the prison population in the 1990s, ensnaring a near majority of young men living in high-poverty neighborhoods, the rate of violent crimes and robberies had begun a large and steady decline, clearly evident by the mid-1990s. Reasons for this drop are contested, but drastic crime reduction seems inconsistent with an exploding prison population. If crimes were decreasing, who was being locked up? One explanation is that a majority of federal and state inmates are serving time for nonviolent offenses.¹ A large share are drug addicts whose afflictions could be treated at less cost and with some hope of success, whereas prison offers none. Full beds in private prisons are also full pockets for the corporations that own these facilities. The monetization of prison bodies resembles in some respects the historical practice of convict leasing; profiting from incarceration creates perverse incentives and powerful lobbies. We have entered an era of virtually unprecedented inequality in access to both wealth and justice. The criminal justice system maps increasingly less well onto the human landscape of antisocial and harmful behavior. Predatory financiers prosper from their crimes while minor drug defendants spend years in prison.

The history of criminalizing African Americans includes special laws, all-white juries, extrajudicial executions, and a massive system of convict leasing. Characterizing black men as dangerous has been used to justify this ill treatment and to stoke politically expedient fears among white people. This history has had a decisive impact on stereotypes about black men and the ongoing disproportionate likelihood they will be convicted of crimes. Seeking liberty was a crime under slavery. Frederick Douglass, who was a runaway slave, famously explained to his audiences that "I appear before you this evening as a thief and a robber. I stole this head, these limbs, this body from my master and ran off with them." In the aftermath of the Civil War, former Confederate states enacted "black codes" designed to restrict and control newly freed slaves. Although many of these were struck down, convict leasing survived challenges and was widely deployed to disarm, disenfranchise, and recapture the labor of freed black men in the post-Reconstruction South. Douglas Blackmon's riveting account of the expansive use of contrived convict labor (*Slavery by Another Name*), and its lasting impact on African American life in the twentieth century, unmasks the constructed narrative and distorted statistics of black crime in the South.² These images play easily into contemporary racial profiling, which results in elevated arrests that further reinforce stereotypes of criminality.

Poverty is a leading correlate of involvement in the criminal justice system, and vice versa. Many felonious perpetrators deserve to be in prison, and we are all safer with them inside. A great many other inmates, however, do not pose a danger and would not be there at all if they were not poor. Aggressive prosecutors and diminished access to effective legal assistance, combined with racially biased policing and sentencing, put poor people of color in a helpless position if they fall into the hands of the law. All along the continuum of involvement with the system—stop, arrest, charge, convict, sentence—African Americans are significantly more likely to receive harsher treatment. This condition, which has long historical roots, has only grown worse in the past generation. Latinos also face harsher treatment than whites, although less severe than African Americans.

Contemporary practices that are discriminatory include stop-and-frisk policing in black and brown neighborhoods, racially profiled traffic stops by municipal police and the highway patrol, "resource officers" in low-income schools who arrest youth for minor infractions and grease the pipeline to prison, and racially disparate arrests and sentencing for drug offenses. Involvement with the criminal justice system is extremely costly, especially for poor people. Fines, fees, court costs, surcharges, and mandated retribution suck money out of the pockets of those who are arrested, convicted, imprisoned, and released. Poor families and friends struggle to find these resources, to enable a visit, phone call, bail, or a decent lawyer. Often the money cannot be raised, and jobs are lost by arrested workers who are stuck in jail. Pressures to plead guilty and accept a sentence are very strong. Going to trial, even if one is innocent, risks a seriously longer sentence than accepting a plea. Families suffer the absence of men in prison. Often they are far away from home, making visits costly and difficult. Once out of prison, an ex-felon's chances of establishing a legal and self-sufficient lifestyle are very bleak. In one form or another, these added costs and ongoing penalties from involvement with the law make the stress of poverty a great deal worse for individuals and families.

Backlash

Over the past fifty years the crime rate in the US first spiked and stayed high for thirty years, and then fell rather dramatically, following a trajectory that criminologists have had a hard time understanding.[3] In the late 1960s crime increased sharply, becoming more violent in response to general disorder and expanded cocaine and heroin trafficking. Black militants, antiwar radicals, and drug-fumed hippie communes defied authority and engaged in various levels of civil disobedience. There were political assassinations, violent confrontations between police and demonstrators, questionable deaths of political activists—all this alongside a growing number of random street crimes, burglaries, auto thefts, and rapes. These societal conditions helped ignite the "culture wars," what Loic Wacquant terms *revanchism,* in which evangelical Christians and conservative politicians mobilized resistance and found wide support among working-class whites. The ethos of justice and equality, or peace and love, was being overcome by fearful concerns about security and punishment. Wacquant's analysis ties the assault on welfare and the war on crime into a dual strategy in the backlash against civil rights, antiwar protests, and emergent women's activism. Welfare had been the more benign method of regulating poor women, making them conform to onerous rules and surrender their dignity in order to qualify for assistance for themselves and their children. Troublesome men were handled through the criminal justice system. As employment shrank, and unskilled black men were increasingly viewed as surplus labor, incarceration exploded. The welfare safety net withered as the carceral web grew and diversified.

The benefits politicians derived from law-and-order rhetoric, along with the growth of private prisons, have spurred a rise in incarceration over the past few decades that places the United States way ahead of the rest of the world in per capita imprisonment. Between 1973 and 2007, the rate of incarceration per 100,000 people in the US increased more than 500 percent.[4] A vastly disproportionate number of current and former inmates are black or brown and poor (70 percent in 2010).[5] Their prospects upon release are crippled by laws and restrictions that make it extremely difficult to resume their lives and contribute to the support of their children. Ex-felons are barred from most federal and state welfare benefits, including housing assistance and financial aid for education. In most states their right to vote has been either delayed or eliminated altogether, and they face an uphill battle in securing any kind of employment. Michelle Alexander's widely cited book, *The New Jim Crow* (2010), likens this condition to the caste status that African Americans experienced prior to the successes of the Civil Rights movement.[6] A professor of law, she focuses on the entrenched class and racial inequities of US criminal justice, and the woeful effect of mass incarceration on black families and their communities. She views these conditions as analogous to the legal and informal restrictions of Jim Crow segregation. Loic Wacquant, a sociologist, strikes a similar theme in his work on racial inequality in the treatment of minorities by the criminal justice system, e.g., *Punishing the Poor* and *Prisons of Poverty*.[7] He traces the punitive turn in US politics to the perceived threat posed by radical civil rights activists and the spate of urban "riots" of the 1960s. The politics of law and order were actively pursued by Reagan and Nixon, including Moynihan's counsel in the Nixon administration. For Wacquant, welfare and criminalization are two sides of the same set of control mechanisms. Beginning in the 1980s, criminal justice grew rapidly in importance, as the backlash against black power and what appeared to be an outbreak of lawlessness fueled the growth of the so-called prison-industrial complex. The stereotype of the inner-city black family included an irresponsible criminal father, a mother who was a welfare queen and likely a prostitute, and children who were truant and delinquent.

Wacquant paints a very bleak picture of the rise in incarceration and the demise of welfare. The relentless drive to punish crime has produced a fiscal quandary, not to mention a threat to democracy:

> Revanchism as public policy toward the dispossessed has thrust the country into a historical cul de sac . . . the spiral of penal escalation has become self-reinforcing as well as self defeating: the carceral Moloch [God who demands sacrifice of children] actively destabilizes the precarious fractions of the postindustrial proletariat it strikes with special zeal, truncates the life options of its members, and further despoils inner-city neighborhoods, thereby reproducing the very social disorders, material insecurity, and symbolic stain it is supposed to alleviate. . . . For the state, the penalization of poverty turns out to be financially ruinous, as it competes with, and eventually consumes, the funds and staff needed to sustain essential public services such as schooling, health, transportation, and social protection.[8]

In other words, we cannot afford the costs of locking up our surplus labor and managing the high level of misery that mass incarceration inflicts on the families and communities of those who are imprisoned. Mass incarceration is expensive. We could send all of those inmates to college for a lot less money. Crime is way down. Do we really need to lock up so many people? And could we really be safer if we are doing nothing to help ex-inmates when they are finally released? Rehabilitation is a thing of the past. Contempt for criminals and stingy impulses by lawmakers and tax payers have virtually eliminated programs in prison that help former inmates change their lives when they get out. The barriers they face cannot be surmounted with only the woefully inadequate help of nonprofits and faith-based out-reach. Not surprisingly, the likelihood of recidivism is high. From whence comes this system that seems so inefficient and mean? Jeremy Travis, Bruce Western, and Steve Redburn offer the following explanation: "The law-and-order issue became a persistent tripwire stretching across national and local politics. Politicians and policy makers increasingly chose to trigger that wire as they sought support for more punitive policies and for expansion of the institutions and resources needed to make good on promises to 'get tough.'"[9]

Most sources agree that the rise of the punitive turn is directly connected to the backlash against the 1960s. Wacquant calls it "revanchism"—revenge and recoupment by political forces who assembled a fear-driven response to the political gains of civil rights. Michelle Alexander views it as the modern arm of a long historical process of racial control. Just as convict leasing was an adjustment to the loss of slave labor, mass incarceration is an adjustment to the legal defeat of Jim Crow. Wacquant dissents from calling it "mass" incarceration, opting instead for the label *hyperincarceration.* He argues that if large numbers of Americans were being locked up at random, if all groups were equally vulnerable, the practice would end quickly. Rather than literally incarcerating the masses, we are incarcerating the black and brown "underclass," whose capacity to resist is severely limited. Unlike when the dogs and fire hoses were turned on civil rights demonstrations and defenseless protesters were viciously attacked on TV, convicted criminals draw scant sympathy and have very little political influence.

In the 1980s many local, state, and federal laws were enacted to increase substantially the punishment for crimes of violence and drug trafficking. Politicians proffered bills, many formulated by the conservative interest group, the American Legislative Exchange Council (ALEC), that removed discretion from judges and prescribed extremely harsh sentences, in some cases for essentially minor drug offenses; increased the length of sentences for many crimes and forbade parole, on the mistaken theory that these measures would serve as a deterrent; and mandated "three strikes" laws that handed down life sentences for repeat offenders, sometimes over relatively minor infractions. The cumulative effect of this muscular escalation in the war on crime and drugs has been to explode the prison system of the nation. These costs are also exploding budgets and posing serious dilemmas in the allocation of public funds.[10]

Another label that has been invoked for this period of rising punish-ment is "neoliberal paternalism." Joe Soss, Richard Fording, and Sanford Schram (2011) also trace the connection, drawn by Wacquant, between the rise of incarceration and the campaign against welfare.[11] They focus on the power of the states in driving early "workfare" experiments that ultimately paved the way for the 1996 federal law (Personal Responsibility and Work Opportunity Act) that drastically altered the welfare safety net. Likewise much of the early increase in sentencing expansions and mandatory mini-mum laws were introduced at the state level, in places where Republican control and ALEC influence were strongest. Neoliberalism refers broadly to governance favoring individualistic free-market values that reward per-sonal achievement and responsibility, and that punish dependency, devi-ance, and failure. Privatization and monetization are related dimensions. Under the neoliberal approach, public services and institutions have been increasingly outsourced, contracted, and/or sold off to private for-profit enterprises. A large share of correctional facilities, personnel, and func-tions have been turned over to private providers, in much the same fashion that other public functions, like waste removal and food service, have been outsourced.

Private corrections corporations, bail bond and parole-monitoring services, and other links in the criminal justice chain ferret out oppor-tunities for collecting fees or deriving other kinds of profit. Two corporations—the GEO Corporation and Corrections Corporation of America (CCA)—have developed huge businesses that combine priva-tized prison operations in many states and lucrative contracts for intern-ing undocumented immigrants. In some states they have sought contracts that guarantee full beds in their facilities—a clause that incentivizes law enforcement to make frivolous arrests and prosecutors to seek long sen-tences. Harsh sentencing laws, which these corporations have supported, increase the stock of monetized bodies sleeping in prison beds. Although the rhetoric of neoliberal paternalism was initially antigovernment/small government, the growth of carceral functions actually has increased the size of government. Privatization has made these operations less account-able, and providers are mainly focused on gleaning profit and extending and hardening the reach of their influence. The profit motive encourages less investment in staff and other cost areas, such as health care and food, and perverse incentives to expand incarceration, which is harmful to the public interest and especially to low-income communities.

Can We All Just Get Along?

Policing directly affects the volume and source of prison inmates. Policing was a key ingredient in the urban disturbances of the 1960s and beyond. The Kerner Commission found that during the 1960s "almost invariably the incident that ignites the disorder arises from police action."[12] More recent high profile disorders were also sparked by police incidents—the 1992 Los Angeles disturbance following the Rodney King verdict and lesser outbreaks in Oakland after the 2010 verdict in the Oscar Grant case.[13] The urban riots of the 1960s planted seeds of revanchism in US politics and policing. Antagonisms between African Americans and police predate the 1960s and are part of old urban struggles in the North over access to patronage jobs, unions, and ethnic succession in neighborhoods; in the South a great many police officers belonged to the Ku Klux Klan. The urban uprisings of the 1960s are generally portrayed as spontaneous out-breaks of rage, usually attributed to rising expectations that were not being met fast enough. This is abstract causation. Behind each was a precipitating event that got the riot underway, and in virtually all cases police played a role in the inception. There was increasing militancy among the Black Pan-thers and the Nation of Islam, and there were acts by the police that were both strategic and spontaneous that aggravated tensions at the neighbor-hood level. FBI and police infiltration of black and antiwar organizations, provocations by police informants, and arrest and murder of activists were part of the era. Street-level interactions were frequently hostile and some-times violent. The incidents that began the several hundred outbreaks of 1964–1968 typically involved police behavior that provoked intense anger among neighbors and bystanders. The outbreaks in 1968 after the assassina-tion of Martin Luther King Jr. are the exception, but they were the apex of the urban violence and the nadir of the nonviolent movement.

The politics of crime and inner-city problems shifted dramatically in the aftermath of the disturbances, both racial and antiwar, and with the presidential defeat of the Democrats in 1968. Crime was on the rise and the ashes of uprisings brought forth calls for more police. Criminology was also evolving from favoring rehabilitation to calling for greater levels of surveillance, arrest, and punishment. In the early 1970s, debate raged over whether convict rehabilitation programs had been successful. A growing consensus found they were not; indeed, they appeared to be a big waste of money and were accused of coddling criminals. In 1974 a large-scale review of 231 studies indicated weak to no results.[14] Under the slogan "nothing works," responding to the query in the title ("What works?"), the verdict was rendered. A major voice in this discussion was James Q. Wilson, whose 1980 article (titled "What works? revisited") reinforced this judgment and promoted punitive alternatives in pursuit of the "deterrent, incapacitative, and retributive purposes of the criminal justice system."[15]

J. Q. Wilson, a longtime friend of Moynihan and a highly influential Harvard policy researcher, was the lead author around the same time on another groundbreaking article in criminology—"Broken Windows: The Police and Neighborhood Safety."[16] The idea was that broken windows in a building signal neglect and invite vandalism. Broken windows in a neighborhood send a more collective message that behavior in this territory is not controlled, that order is not enforced. Wilson and coauthor George Kelling argued that crime control begins with the small stuff, the "quality of life" offenses that disturb the serenity of the neighborhood environment, like beggars and scary-looking youth who hang out on sidewalks. They argue that as the neighborhood becomes more threatening and less family-friendly, residents pull inside and do not establish effective social cohesion. These anomic conditions feed on themselves, eroding the local social order in neighborhoods. The answer that Wilson and Kelling recommended was aggressive proactive policing: eliminate tolerance for minor infractions, like littering, graffiti, or boisterous behavior; arrest panhandlers, street vendors, and prostitutes; stop and frisk passersby who appear to be suspicious; restore order and establish visible authority. This idea had considerable vindictive appeal, and as crime prevention that justified expansion of police powers and personnel.

The most prominent example of broken-windows policing was in New York City under Mayor Rudolph Giuliani, who fully embraced this idea in the 1990s. New York became a showcase for crime reduction that was attributed to this new "zero tolerance" approach. Crime did fall dramatically in New York under this regime, a fact that seemed to confirm the value of the concept and program. However, crime fell dramatically in cities across the United States, including many where the broken-windows theory had not affected policing. Research was casting doubt on the validity of the concept. Robert Sampson and Stephen Raudenbush published two important articles that reported findings on broken windows, one in 1999 and another in 2004. The earlier article questioned whether signs of disorder actually cause more crime, or if they are simply concurrent, reflections of the same underlying cause. In an extensive analysis they found little support for the thesis, except small effects for robberies. Their 2004 study further undercut the premise of broken windows, finding that perceived black occupancy in a neighborhood, not physical signs of disorder, offered the best predictor of crime concerns among respondents. They concluded that "it may well be that reducing actual levels of disorder will not remedy psychological discomfort, for that discomfort stems from more insidious sources [i.e., racial aversion]."[17]

The potential for racial disparity in broken-windows policing (also known as "zero tolerance policing" (ZTP) was a topic in research reported by Bernard Harcourt and Jens Ludwig in 2006, titled "Reefer Madness."[18] They analyzed misdemeanor arrests for marijuana possession in New York City from 1989 to 2000, encompassing the period when Giuliani was mayor. They found that introduction of ZTP resulted in a dramatic increase in annual arrests for this offense; from only 10 in 1993, the year prior, to 644 in 2000. African Americans and Latinos accounted for 85 percent of the arrests but only 50 percent of the population. Compared with whites, black and brown arrestees fared worse at every step in the post-arrest process. The analysis also indicated that, contrary to the hoped-for reduction of violent crime in heavily policed neighborhoods, areas with large numbers of marijuana misdemeanor convictions also had increases in violent crimes. Other New York neighborhoods were experiencing less crime, but the stop and frisk marijuana shakedowns that predominantly occurred in minority areas were instead associated with a rising incidence of violence. "An increase in MPV [marijuana in public view] arrests over the period translates into an *increase* [italics in original] in serious crime— not, as the broken window theory would predict, a decrease in serious crime. This is exactly the opposite of what we would want . . . [and] suggests that this policing strategy focused on misdemeanor MPV arrests is having exactly the wrong effect on serious crime—increasing it, rather than decreasing it."[19]

Harcourt and Ludwig addressed the legal strategies needed to argue the discriminatory effects of this practice. They were not optimistic that the very high threshold of showing racially discriminatory "intent" (*Washington v. Davis*, 1976) could be met. However, a class action suit over this practice did make it to court in 2013; federal Judge Shira Scheindlin ruled in *Floyd, et al v. City of New York* that the overly aggressive "stop and frisk" behavior of New York City police, combined with clear practices of racial profiling, was unconstitutional and a violation of Fourth Amendment protections against unwarranted search and seizure.[20] The number of stops had reached into the hundreds of thousands, with the vast majority done in minority neighborhoods to minority youth and men. The take from these encounters was meager; fewer than 4 percent of stops actually resulted in arrest.[21] Misdemeanor arrests that did occur, especially for marijuana, proved to be costly for those arrested and part of a process of criminalization that has fed the engine of mass/hyperincarceration. Initial involvement over a minor arrest creates a record, might cause a lost job, and leaves a bitter experience with police and justice. The rude intrusions suffered by neighborhood residents have contributed to general hostility toward the police that in turn produces uncooperative witnesses and relationships not conducive to preventing and solving crimes. A frequent editorial complaint about the residents of inner-city, mostly black neighborhoods is that they do not cooperate with police. The behavior of police that produces such anger and suspicion is rarely mentioned in these arguments.

Police justifications for making such large numbers of stops in nonwhite areas are cloaked in the logic of broken windows, and statistics showing where the most crimes occur (the "hot spots"). In the *Floyd* case the city argued they were pursuing crime where they know it happens, and that they tended to stop nonwhites because they are more commonly the perpetrators a "statistical racism" reason to permit racial profiling and a self-fulfilling prediction about where arrests occur. (College dorms, for example, might be fruitful sites to make marijuana arrests, but these are rare.) The actual motives behind the stops, the critical need to show racist intent, were brought out in the case by witnesses, both police and civilians, and some documents that confirmed explicit racial profiling and strongly indicated the use of quotas for stops and arrests. The marijuana arrests were particularly insidious. The law in New York permits possession of small amounts of marijuana if it is concealed; once it is in public view, possession becomes a misdemeanor. When persons who have been stopped must empty their pockets, possession may instantly convert from decriminalized to a misdemeanor, subject to arrest and fine. So the main net effect of this type of policing is to drag large numbers of low-income minority youth into the criminal justice system, brand them and initiate/enhance rap sheets, and further impoverish their families. Although minority youth are the ones who get arrested for using and selling marijuana, they are slightly less likely either to use or sell the drug than their white counterparts, who rarely get arrested for the same offenses.[22] And these arrests, proceedings, and damaging criminal records are doing nothing to reduce serious crimes in the neighborhoods where these kids and their families live. If Harcourt and Ludwig are correct, these practices actually may be making serious crime worse. They are certainly increasing tensions between the police and a great many people who live in these communities, conditions that detract from effective crime control and undermine the perceived legitimacy of law enforcement.

Youth growing up in overpoliced neighborhoods have a very hard time staying out of trouble and finishing school. Victor Rios, a sociologist, published an ethnography about these problems in black and Latino neighborhoods of Oakland, California.[23] He did an extended study of the lives of low-income youth and the unmanageable challenges they face from police surveillance and harassment. As individuals, they are stereotyped and lumped together, ripe for arrest whenever they are out in the street. Rios describes what he terms a "youth control complex" that also includes schools, recreation centers, and even parents in a web of punitive discipline. The effects have been pervasively negative, and extend into most corners of youth existence in the places where this occurs. Police are often stationed at neighborhood recreation centers and seek the cooperation of center staff in providing information and gate keeping against youth they have targeted. Neighborhood recreation centers are supposed to protect kids from involvement with the law, but they are also part of an institutionalized process that leads them to prison.

The Pipeline to Prison

Schools are one of the most intense sites of youth criminalization. School shootings by white kids in mostly white places like Colorado and Newtown, Connecticut have militarized US schools, in poor neighborhoods especially, with in-house police labeled "resource officers," and rigid zero-tolerance regimes whose logic is similar to broken windows. Schools have become hardened sites with armed police officers who brook no disturbance. Name-calling, scuffling, swearing, and especially fighting are offenses that can lead to arrest. Security and discipline in inner-city schools have been outsourced to the police, with the result that a great many children are being arrested, charged, and in some cases jailed for doing things that used to get kids sent to the principal's office. A seven-year-old girl in St. Petersburg, Florida was arrested and dragged away in handcuffs for throwing a tantrum. The cuffs kept sliding off her little wrists. She was African American, as are the majority of the children arrested and the escalating number suspended from school. The US Department of Education released a report in March 2014 that detailed the extensive number of disciplinary actions taken against nonwhite students at all grade levels. Even in preschools, black children were 18 percent of enrollment but 42 percent of those suspended at least one time; 48 percent of the black children had been suspended more than once. At higher grades the disparities were found to be even greater, but the realization that this process begins with such young children is chilling. Disparate and counterproductive disciplinary practices prompted the Departments of Justice and Education to release jointly developed guidelines intended to limit and mitigate the effects of zero-tolerance policies in schools.[24] Dismantling or reforming this regime will not be easy.

Rios's accounts of the boys in his study and their experiences in school reveal the dynamics that cause so many to lose interest and drop out. His narratives also flesh out the process whereby experiences in school replicate those on the street and in other public spaces that, taken together, limit and stigmatize their identities and capacity to act. He describes what has come to be known as the "school to prison pipeline." This pathway has been reported for youth of color in many other cities and has become a subject of growing concern.[25] In the work we have done in Tampa, Florida this damaging process was very evident. One of the neighborhoods described briefly in chapter 4, where a large number of former public housing residents were relocated, became the site of extended ethnographic research by members of the team.

Lance Arney, my former doctoral student (now Dr. Arney), has spent nearly a decade working with youth in this neighborhood, within the context of a youth arts program that originated with two brothers whose family had deep roots in the neighborhood. In 1984 they founded an organization (I am calling it "Obadiah") designed to involve young black kids in art and nature, and to divert them from the dangers posed by drugs and police. We got involved in 2007, when they were about to lose the property where classes were held and one of the founders had become gravely ill. Through the university we were able to provide student volunteers and other small resources, assistance that helped them keep going. Lance became the interim director when the brother who was ill became increasingly frail and passed away in November 2008. The organization included a large following of youth who were teens and younger. Many were relatives of the founders, or their friends, or the kids of their parents' friends, or others who heard about the Obadiah programs. It was a large loose network of mostly low-income black people who lived in the neighborhood. When the founder, a well-regarded folk artist, was alive the kids did various kinds of art projects and were engaged in lessons about black history, nature, and black spirituality. His passing left a large void, but his brother and adult relatives, other community members who admired his work, and students and faculty at USF were able to maintain operations and ultimately obtain new space and added resources that have allowed the organization to continue to exist, although just barely.

Over nearly a decade, we have witnessed young boys suffer through adolescence, grow into young adulthood and mostly end up in prison, or homeless, or both in sequence. As was described by Rios, these kids are prime targets for police harassment. The neighborhood is considered a high-crime zone, or a hot spot in current parlance. It is one of the poorest areas in the city and it has the largest proportion of children under 18. A SWAT team patrols the neighborhood in cruisers, and drug shakedowns are frequent. Helicopters often can be heard overhead on many days and nights. Obadiah has been a place where kids can temporarily avoid the hazards of the street and sidewalk, do enjoyable activities, and not be treated like thugs. During Lance's research, Tampa's mayor hired a police chief who favored broken-windows policing. Obadiah's neighborhood was a heavily targeted area, and many of the kids he worked with ended up on a police list dubbed "The Worst of the Worst." Many had been arrested in the past for minor offenses, nuisance charges, and in a few cases serious criminal acts. To the extent that arrest records determined who was on the list, it would have been a very long list. Few teens in that neighborhood were able to avoid scrapes with police. For kids on the list, life in the neighborhood was filled with conflictual encounters. The following extended excerpt from Arney's dissertation illustrates the tenor and effects of these interactions.[26]

> Youth have told me that the cops make threats to them such as, "We're not going to stop arresting you guys until we've cleaned out the entire neighborhood." I ask Malcolm if the police say anything to him like that.

"Yeah, they said things like, yeah, all the time, all the time, 'We gonna have all y'all in jail.' . . . You're not doing nothing wrong. When you're just sitting there, you're standing somewhere, or you on the block or on the street corner or you somewhere like at a friend's house in their yard. These officers' ego is big enough to just approach you like you a criminal and like they know you because they've been talking to other officers about you. And they want to arrest you and they want to get you and they want to criminalize you. They want to do this, they want to—and they don't have reasons to, but they try to all the time."

Another youth, Dante, described to me how he began to be targeted by the police after he got out of a juvenile offender program when he was 14:

"When I got out I went back to [the neighborhood], and it was like all the police knew me. So every time one of them seen me they would harass me, take me to jail about dumb shit, talking about sticker [a trespass warning notice] on the house, so they [the police] jump out and then took me to jail, talking about I was trespassing. So it got so bad that we would go to the park to hang out. They came to the park fucking with us. So my mama got sick of them fucking with me. She called [the police department's] Internal Affairs but they still ain't do nothing. . . . So when they start to come to our park, we left there. I hate the police. . . . When they would take me to jail, I would beat the case sometime 'cause they was all lies."[27]

Youth described to me in great detail encounters they had had with police; incidents of surveillance, detainment, questioning, being taken into custody, and arrest; as well as tactics and strategies used by law enforcement to claim probable cause for arresting them or alleging that they had violated the terms of their sanctions or probation. Sometimes, nonviolent crimes such as possession or sale of illegal substances, or property crimes such as robberies and burglaries, had in fact occurred and they were indeed guilty. Other times, youth were charged or ticketed for very petty offenses, such as jaywalking or riding too slowly on a bicycle, "offenses" which at times were used as probable cause for a search. There were also, according to how the youth described the incidents, many instances in which false arrests were made and "crimes" were reportedly fabricated or instigated by the police, and instances in which police used excessive force or violence for no legally justifiable reason.

The ordinary activities of walking down the sidewalk, crossing the street, and riding a bike were cause for traffic violations cited against [neighborhood] youth. Walking down the street could be described by police as "failure to use sidewalk," even where there were no sidewalks, "obstructing traffic," even when there were no cars on the road, or "pedestrian traffic in the wrong direction," if walking on the side of a street—or sidewalk—in the direction counter to the traffic on that side. Numerous citations are related to bicycle riding: riding without the use of hands, riding without proper lights or reflectors, riding too slowly, failure to use arm gesture turn signals, and failure to maintain proper distance from another vehicle. The accusation could easily be made that a bike was one that had been stolen, and then it could be confiscated. Traffic violations were often used as probable cause for a search, and if a pocketknife or cannabis cigarette, for example, were found on the youth, an arrest would be made for possession of a "concealed/deadly weapon" or possession of cannabis. Traffic citations are costly, and I know individual youth who owe thousands of dollars in citations to the traffic court. Unpaid traffic citations make it impossible for the youth to obtain a driver's license if they do not already have one; unpaid citations will lead to the suspension, revocation, or cancellation of a driver's license if they already do. This, in turn, can lead to future arrests—and jail time—for operating a motor vehicle without a license or with license cancelled, suspended, or revoked if the youth are caught driving a motor vehicle on the road.[28]

The experiences of these kids were of relentless baiting, hassling and frequent arrests. They had similar experiences at school, where the resource officers also seemed to have a list. These are the links that connect kids to prison through a metaphorical pipeline that apparently starts in preschool. Once in it, escape is difficult and options are few. It is a demoralizing way to spend childhood and adolescence, and it is also materially disabling. The multiple citations described above for what seem like frivolous offenses can rack up huge fines and penalties, costs their families cannot afford, and prevent kids from maintaining legal driver's licenses. Without a car, it is hard to hold a job in Tampa. Without a job there is little hope of paying the fines that continue to multiply with addition of penalties for late and non-payments. Poverty and the criminal justice system are in an abusive relationship. The fees, fines, and other charges that can be cadged from poor people under pressure of going to jail are part of a neoliberal shift from taxing the rich to fining the poor. Entangling enforceable debt with the criminal justice system has opened the door to debtors prisons, and is literally criminalizing poverty.

Debt Is the Poverty Trap

The end of Reconstruction in the late nineteenth-century South led to new forms of enslavement based on debt. Sharecroppers in agriculture and wage workers in various industries lived in quarters owned by their employers, bought necessities on credit in stores owned by their employers, and were often unable to calculate, let alone challenge, the amount they were due for their labor versus what they owed in credit charges. When the latter was deemed to exceed the former, which was invariably the case, the tenant was stuck for another season. Failure to pay debts or fines was the preferred pretext for incarceration under the convict leasing system. Often the charges behind the fines were simply concocted for non offenses like loitering or vagrancy. Hundreds of thousands of black men in most of the southern states were swept up in this net. In court, their fines were paid by contractors who then sold them to work off their debts in the mines, mills, turpentine stills, or plantations where owners needed labor. This innovation in labor procurement helped resuscitate southern industries and created huge family fortunes for the owners. Not good for the inmates, however, whose sentences were long and conditions extremely harsh. The death rate was high, especially in mines and steel mills.[29] Although these ghastly conditions hopefully will remain a thing of the past, debt bondage and convict leasing are being reinvented.

At every step, from initial arrest through conviction, sentencing, serving time, release, and post-release supervision of parole or probation, fines and fees are levied against the accused/inmate/parolee. The financial collapse of 2008 brought revenue crises in state and local governments. A common solution to the problem was to raise existing fees and fines, sometimes drastically, and institute new ones. Those in the criminal justice system have fallen especially hard on poor people. "Legal financial obligations" (LFOs) refer to the exactions made of persons who are involved in court or criminal proceedings. In addition to fines for offenses and/or fees associated with adjudication, this category includes other legal payment demands (like child support or restitution), tracked through increasingly sophisticated, linked databases. These payments can be automatically deducted from, and hugely deplete, a paycheck before it is even received.[30] The revenues from these practices are viewed as morally justifiable returns that help the courts continue to function during hard budget times. However, the costs of collecting the fees they are owed, plus the costs of reincarcerating parolees who cannot afford to pay, apparently exceed the return.[31] The fee amount calculators operate independent of the subject's ability to pay. The sums owed are often very substantial.

A great many people have LFO debts so large they will never be able to retire them, and intrusions from these obligations will plague them long after their sentences have been completed. Prisoners with children continue to incur child support obligations while they serve. Money they might earn from a job in the prison industries sector will be applied to that demand, but their earnings can be as little as twelve cents an hour, and nowhere is it close to minimum wage. With that kind of deficit, a short sentence with an average obligation will yield many thousands of dollars in debt that leaves prison with the inmate at release, along with all the other unpaid charges that accrued from the time of initial arrest.[32] Release brings new added fees; costs of drug tests, fees to the parole officer, mandatory classes, and other charges that are connected with being on parole or probation. Under terms of release, prompt payments must be maintained on LFO debt, or the parolee/debtor can be returned to prison. Collection in many places has been turned over to private agencies, who may relentlessly pursue and harass parolees in arrears, and can get them ordered back to prison if they do not, or cannot, pay. The criteria for proving inability to pay are almost impossible to meet, and LFO debts cannot be dismissed in bankruptcy. This activity surfaces in background checks and credit reports. Bad credit scores, like criminal records, make it hard to get a job. But if your paycheck gets eaten before you get it, having a job is not a solution anyway, even if you are lucky enough to get one.

Holzer (2009) has suggested that the upside-down math in the LFO payment equation encourages withdrawing from the labor force and resorting to underground illegal sources of income.[33] One woman interviewed by Mary Katzenstein and Mitali Nagrecha said she had considered prostitution as a way to earn off-the-books income that could let her finally get free of her LFOs. The loan shark is the state and its private partners, who circle around people who fall into this trap and keep them continually off balance and literally unable to get ahead or rejoin society.

Stress has been identified as a principal side effect and aggravator of poverty. One of the stated goals of broken-windows policing was to eliminate stress-inducing and aversive conditions in public spaces of certain neighborhoods. Massively stopping and arresting people for the minor offenses described in the theory of broken windows appears, however, to have become a major escalator of stress within the resident populations of places where it is done. This large increase in arrests, combined with the rise of punitive revenue strategies, has further immiserated people who were already struggling, and the enormous costs have destabilized fiscal conditions at all levels of government. The emergent literature on the effects of LFOs is virtually unanimous in the verdict that these practices are bad for society. Mass incarceration, mandatory long sentences, and the shameless fleecing of the indigent are all having bad effects, not only on the poor but also on the competing demands of the budget and the broader purposes of government.

Affluenza

Although the poor have been subjected to unprecedented levels of attention by the criminal justice system—and the war on drugs has ballooned the prisons with young nonwhite nonviolent low-income offenders—white collar crime, committed mostly by elite white actors, has virtually disappeared. Not that it no longer occurs, but many of the behaviors that used to count as illegal insider trading, fraud, or corrupt practices have been effectively decriminalized by the power of the corporate/financial sector in relation to the lawmaking and enforcement sectors.[34] When the savings and loan scandal erupted in the late 1980s, inflicting billions in damages and causing untold losses of jobs and investments, nearly a thousand elite perpetrators went to prison. The 2008 financial meltdown, often referred to as the "Great Recession," which caused far greater and more long-lasting damage than the S&L crimes, has resulted in virtually no criminal charges against high-level managers responsible for what happened. Bonuses and salaries of CEOs have risen sharply; the stock market also has soared, and inequality of wealth in the United States has reached an extraordinary level. Bad behavior on Wall Street appears to have been repaid with unparalleled rewards. Due to the fraudulent and reckless actions of these same people, several million people lost their jobs in the real economy. More than nine million houses have been foreclosed with more still in the pipeline.

The financial crimes just described represent pathology on a very large scale. Due to willful misconduct and excessive greed on the part of identifiable individuals on Wall Street, millions of people have been severely harmed. Foreclosure is a wrenching experience for a family: kids lose belongings, friends, pets, and peace of mind; parents lose much of what they had accumulated and suffer bad credit and scorn; and marriages often break up over the stress of the process. For the many who were duped and defrauded, it is not too different from having your life savings stolen in a robbery, except if that had happened, neighbors would sympathize and the police might try to arrest the perpetrator. The financial crisis of 2008, spurred by the massive collapse of fraudulent securitized mortgages, was not a natural disaster. It was a man-made train wreck, and the men who made it (most were men) escaped without punishment. The contradiction between impunity and forgiveness for the big league robbers on Wall Street and relentless punishment for poor youths living in inner-city hot spots has not gone unnoticed. A growing number of commentators and journalists have focused on the Dickensian quality of the contemporary "two-tiered" US justice system and the extraordinary rise in wealth inequality, not seen since the Gilded Age of the original robber barons.[35] Mass incarceration of the poor juxtaposes ironically, almost cartoonishly, against the meteoric rise of wealth and power among the corporate criminals who maneuvered and manipulated financial markets and colluded to steal trillions of dollars.

Ruby Payne, a reputed expert on poverty who will be discussed in the next chapter, claims that the rich have a distinct culture, that the rules they live by are different from the rules the rest of us follow. Research tends to confirm that observation. To the extent that there is a "culture of wealth" that mirrors the alleged "culture of poverty," it is a set of values and a design for living thick with tangled pathology. A growing body of research has shown disproportionate sociopathic and psychopathic tendencies among people who have wealth and power. A recent study by social psychologists Michael Kraus and Dacher Keltner found that wealthy respondents are likely to believe that wealthy people are genetically superior, and that their own elevated social positions are inherently well deserved.[36] They are less sympathetic than nonwealthy people are with the sick or unfortunate. They are more in favor of punishing rather than rehabilitating criminal offenders, and they view those below them in the social order as morally inferior to themselves. They have a much stronger belief that society and the economy, as they are, are fair and just. Other researchers have reported similar clusters of what Kraus and Keltner term "essentialist" thinking. Paul Piff, a Berkeley psychologist who collaborates with Keltner (also at

Berkeley), has conducted both naturalistic and laboratory experiments designed to probe the shared ethos of the rich. In a series of seven studies, Piff and his colleagues found that, "Upper-class individuals behave more unethically than lower class individuals . . . were more likely to break the law while driving [studies 1 & 2] . . . exhibit unethical decision-making tendencies [study 3], take valued goods from others [study 4], lie in a negotiation [study 5], cheat to increase their chances of winning a prize [study 6], and endorse unethical behavior at work [study 7]."[37]

They have found that wealthy respondents are more likely to view greed as socially beneficial, and they are less likely to register empathy or concern than lower income viewers of a video about children with cancer. In a study conducted at a pedestrian crosswalk they found that drivers of expensive cars were significantly less likely to yield to a pedestrian trying to cross than were drivers of cheaper cars. They also cite surveys of charitable contributions indicating that the wealthy give relatively far less than lower income donors.[38] They also cite findings that wealthy people are not good at reading social cues, tend to be more disengaged during social interactions, and are generally more focused on themselves. Piff speculates that wealth confers the luxury of not having to care what others think or feel.

In related research, a group of clinical psychologists have reviewed research and other evidence on the personality characteristics of white collar criminals. They examine the corporate personalities and official pronouncements and actions behind three recent incidents of major corporate wrongdoing—the Gulf oil spill of 2010, avoidance of recalling dangerous vehicles made by Toyota in 2009, and crimes of the financial industry revealed in 2008.[39] They cite numerous examples of behaviors and expressed motivations that conform to accepted definitions of psychopathy. Another research group following a similar track surveyed a group of 203 corporate professionals and found they had significantly higher scores on the standard checklists for psychopathy than the general population.[40] Two members of this team (Paul Babiak and Robert Hare) wrote a popular book about their research, titled *Snakes in Suits*, which examines the larger context of corporate culture and the reward structures that attract and promote individuals who suffer from the following characteristics: "This group, the subject of this book, displays a personality disorder rooted in lying, manipulation, deceit, egocentricity, callousness, and other potentially destructive traits. This personality disorder, one of the first to be described in the psychiatric literature, is psychopathy."[41]

The subtitle of this section of this chapter, "affluenza," refers to an alleged psychiatric disorder invoked in defense of a remorseless sixteen-year-old Texas youth who had killed four people and injured twelve in a drunken car crash. At his trial for intoxicated manslaughter his lawyer argued that he was the victim of a pathological upbringing by his extremely wealthy parents. They denied him nothing and set no limits on his behavior; they failed to hold him responsible for his past mistakes and infractions; and they neglected his moral education. Use of the term *affluenza*, was nontechnical, as it turned out. *The Diagnostic and Statistical Manual of Mental Disorders*, the encyclopedia of certified psychiatric maladies, does not include it. Its prior meaning was associated with anticonsumerism, and those who lament materialism and "keeping up with the Joneses." Converting it into a form of psychopathic illness was a stretch his lawyer later admitted. In issuing her opinion, the judge disclaimed any influence from that argument, but her ruling was extraordinarily benign. The youth was put on probation for ten years and sentenced to an extremely expensive youth rehab facility in Newport Beach, California, that his parents agreed to pay for. Many commentators expressed doubt that a low-income black kid would have fared this well, and many examples of cases where they did not, including a sentence handed down by this same judge, were offered in illustration. Although affluenza may be a mythical and tendentious concept, belief in the pathological upbringing of most poor black youth is both widespread and embraced by respected academics. Why not exculpate those who are convicted of crimes and send them all to expensive retreats for rehabilitation?

When poverty researchers call for an expanded emphasis on culture, they rarely mean to include the cultural beliefs and practices of those who actually have power to achieve the ends they seek. The rich have abundant choices, but they are rarely punished for the bad ones they make. Where is the correction for the moral hazard that causes such errors? Why is there so little attention paid to the norms, values, learned behaviors, and beliefs about their own entitlement that characterize the shared culture of the rich? Their social isolation, cutthroat competition, and ideological selfishness may give rise to collectively dysfunctional social and cultural norms. Perhaps we need policies that encourage them to share their good fortune and care more about their fellow citizens, much as we design programs to encourage poor people to get married and do a better job of managing their finances.

The most damaging element in stereotypes about black people—especially those who are young, poor, and male—is a presumption of inherent criminality. Moynihan's analysis of the straight line between single mothers and delinquent children provided an apparently respectable explanation for this long-held prejudice. He is often cited in this connection, and his writing on the subject was calculably fear-inducing. He achieved instant fame for his contribution to public opinion about the Watts uprising in 1965. He returned to themes of crime and unrest often in the years that followed, although he did object from the floor of the Senate during the Reagan/Bush/Clinton years when the mass incarceration machine was roaring ahead.

Surveys of employers suggest that the criminalization of blackness is firmly rooted in a sector where it really matters. Employers of unskilled and low-skilled labor cite it often as a reason not to hire black workers. Indeed, this prejudice is so strong that it trumps an actual criminal record for a white applicant, who often will be hired over a comparably qualified blemish-free black applicant. For black applicants who do have criminal records, their prospects are virtually hopeless. The acceleration of what Wacquant has called the "punitive turn" has brought deep misery to African American communities in all parts of the United States. Some states are worse than others; the Sunbelt unsurprisingly leads in substandard justice and very harsh treatment. Alongside the growth in convictions for nonviolent offenses that can carry harsh sentences, has been the rise of private prisons. Corporate incentives to increase incarcerations and cut costs of oversight and services have had a deleterious effect on our justice system, and on the literally millions of inmates who are warehoused for very long terms and are unemployable on release.

At the other end of the social spectrum are the very wealthy, who have grown more so during the same period that incarceration of the lower classes was exploding. Their direct misdeeds in the derivatives market and in inveigling/bribing elected officials to buy into fraudulent investments masquerading as AAA securities are only part of the role their wealth has played in the creation of poverty among the growing "underclass" and the previously middle-class.

6

Commercializing the Culture of Poverty

• • • • • • • • • • • • • • • • • •

> Generational Poverty has its own culture, hidden rules, and belief systems. . . . Often the attitude in generational poverty is that society owes one a living.
> —Ruby Payne, *A Framework for Understanding Poverty*

> The biggest difference between us and white folks is that we know when we are playing [lying].
> —Alberta Roberts, quoted in John Langston Gwaltney, *Drylongso*

The main reason for identifying poverty's causes is to find ways to alleviate its effects or even eliminate it altogether. Are there reliable policy options that will enable poor people to escape their condition and enter onto the path to prosperity? The fiftieth anniversary of LBJ's declaration of the War on Poverty (in early 1964) revived the long-running dispute over whether the antipoverty programs of the 1960s have worked. Many pundits claimed they had been a failure. It is true that we still have a lot of poverty, but none of the major Great Society programs ever has been adequately funded in relation to need, and many have suffered reduction or elimination over the years.[1] It also has been shown that we would have a lot more poverty now if it were not for the expansion of Social Security and Medicare, which have kept millions of seniors out of poverty, and other popular programs like Head Start, which offers safe child care for low-income working mothers. These programs have survived because they are popular, but they are under constant pressure from fiscal conservatives and those opposed to any kind of government-funded social safety net.

Ideological conflicts over poverty policy have evolved over the past three decades in a decidedly neoliberal direction. Increasingly, poverty has been viewed as an individual problem that can be solved only by individuals making changes that enable their ascension into the middle class—gaining new skills or overcoming impediments like addiction. The emphasis is on helping people one at a time learn how to be middle-class, to achieve proper motivation and decorum, and thus to win acceptance by employers and others who can be helpful in attaining a better life. To break the cycle of poverty, it is also deemed necessary to improve parenting and develop supportive programs for children so that they do not follow their parents' example into their own adulthood. This individualized approach has become the predominant model for antipoverty programming. The presumed cause of the problem is cultural pathology, not material scarcity. Viewed in the aggregate, this approach is both Sisyphean and inherently competitive. While parenting classes were underway at the neighborhood community center, the recession was killing the jobs of those in the class. Among graduates of self-improvement or retraining programs, competition for jobs, especially good jobs, is intense. Most participants cannot win. Those who do make good poster material, and those who don't serve the purpose of demonstrating how hard it is to help "these people."

When the Office of Economic Opportunity (OEO) was formed in the summer of 1964, the preferred model for combating poverty was "community action" and "maximum feasible participation." The plan was to fight poverty together, to form neighborhood brigades and local organizations that would animate reform, devise programs, and agitate for greater fairness and opportunity. Funding for organized self-help and grassroots ingenuity would create new collective ladders out of poverty and new institutions for civic involvement. Grants were made directly to community organizations, some too hastily vetted, deliberately bypassing local government officials. It was a volatile period in which to be promoting grassroots organizing. In many cities, the Civil Rights movement seemed to be morphing into armed confrontation between police and Black Panthers, and a string of urban disturbances erupted during the same period the community action plans were coming into place. Conservative politicians blamed OEO grantees for abetting these uprisings, apparently without justification, but they made convenient targets and a good wedge. Leadership training for the grantees followed an approach developed by the Chicago community organizer, Saul Alinsky, who favored confrontation and angry agitation. Local politicians disliked having garbage dumped on their driveways and other such direct actions. Within a year, the community action approach had been effectively scrapped by OEO, a casualty of intense multipronged political pressure. Alice O'Connor cites a *New York Times* reporter from that period who said: "Mr. Shriver [Sargent Shriver, the director] and his Office of Economic Opportunity have inherited a thousand local political fights."[2] Notably, Moynihan opposed community action approaches. He published a book in 1969, *Maximum Feasible Misunderstanding*, in which he strongly criticized the program.[3]

Moynihan's 1965 report, refocusing the poverty problem onto broken families and off of corrupt and inattentive local politicians, arrived during a shift already underway against organized solutions to the structural causes of poverty, and in favor of individualized approaches to resocializing and retraining culturally deficient poor people. Moynihan made no specific policy recommendations in his report, but his diagnosis of the problem opened space for others to develop therapeutic and pedagogical programs designed to cure the culture of poverty. This orientation favored provision of services over income transfer, and it encouraged the development of what Theresa Funicello labeled the "Poverty Industry."[4] With the expansive growth of private nonprofit agencies and foundations, and the increased privatization of social welfare and penal functions, entrepreneurism also has blossomed. Some of the figures involved in the marriage promotion programs discussed in chapter 3 have been very adept at developing business models, and many similar niches can be identified and filled in the "neoliberal paternalistic" campaign to fix people suffering from poverty. Poverty has spawned an industry wherein a significant share of the funds slated for alleviation are actually diverted to individuals who are comfortable—professionals of various sorts and entrepreneurs who have discovered how to profit from demand for solutions for this problem. One lucrative example was the omnibus education bill, *No Child Left Behind* (NCLB), signed into law by President Bush in 2002, which defined low-income minority students as particular targets of reform. Public schools were mandated to develop strategies for increasing the educational success of poor kids, especially those who are African American and/or Latino. This requirement created a need for programmatic solutions and professional development for teachers and others directly involved in the education of this very difficult targeted group. Grants from the government and a growing number of wealthy philanthropists allocated sizable sums for these purposes.

The pejorative term *poverty pimp* has long-standing provenance, but an ambiguous meaning. For conservatives, it is generally applied to middle-class civil rights activists and left-wing academics involved in programs, political action, or funded research about poverty. A very different usage could apply to individuals who capitalize on stereotypes and beliefs about the culture of poverty, entrepreneurs who profit from assuaging the discomfort of middle-class teachers and practitioners about the demeanor and appearance of low-income students, parents, and clients. Cultural explanations for poverty have spawned a cornucopia of consultants, some of whom earn large sums from workshops and training products purporting to explain and/or alter the nature and culture of people who are poor. This chapter addresses that manifestation.

The most successful of these enterprises is called "aha! Process, Inc." Founded by Ruby Payne, a former school administrator, this system is explicitly based on the contention that poor, middle-class, and wealthy individuals practice very different cultures—operate by what she calls "the hidden rules of class." To work effectively with poor people it is important to know their culture, including their very different cognitive orientations and capacities. The family is the cradle of social learning in this model, the self-perpetuating instigator of "intergenerational poverty" for those who are raised by poor parents and live in the midst of other poor people. The challenge for educators is first to understand the depth and importance of these cultural differences, and then find ways to reeducate their low-income students into the beliefs, values, and behavior of the middle class. Payne's book *A Framework for Understanding Poverty* (henceforth referred to as *Framework*) has sold well over a million copies since it first came out in 1996, and her lectures and workshops have earned many millions of dollars. Her website, ahaprocess.com, contains literally dozens of products that can be purchased and services that can be requisitioned. "Aha" refers to the reaction of her typically middle-class audiences when they discover that their preconceptions about the deficiencies of poor people were right all along. Conventional stereotypes are real, they are told. The cause of the poverty problem resides in misdirected values, lack of impulse control, and a general inability to plan or organize. The culture of poverty thesis is the underlying basis of this system; she explicitly cites Oscar Lewis. Her workshops, lectures, products, and persona have been hugely successful.

In an era of accountability and "evidence-based" programming, Payne's is remarkably evidence-free. A self-published author, she describes herself as "the leading US expert on the mindsets of poverty, middle class, and wealth."[5] Although she does have a PhD, she is not trained as a researcher. Her professed expertise on poverty derives solely from personal experiences of having been married to a man whose family was poor, and having served as principal of an elementary school in a very wealthy district. It is worth noting that Ruby and her (now former) husband are both white. The "data" she offers are her own observations, which she sets forth as "truth claims," along with a set of fictional vignettes she has crafted that allegedly convey the behavior, thought patterns, and personalities of poor people. She claims to be color-blind, but these narratives are laced with ethnic stereotypes. They follow a playbook of racist images and essentially confirm the view of poor people put forth in writing by Charles Murray and many media and print commentators. The pejorative nature of these images is cloaked in concern for the well-being of children. Teachers need to understand realistically the difficulties involved in teaching kids from poor families, it is argued, to understand the very large gap of class and culture that separates the average school teacher from her students who come from impoverished families. With that understanding firmly in mind, while they are trying to teach them math, reading, geography, and/or history, they should also implement instruction in how to pretend to be middle-class.

Payne's system is unapologetically assimilationist. If poor students want to succeed as adults they need to unlearn the culture of their families and learn anew how to think, talk, and act like middle-class kids. Her conception of poverty is exclusively centered on the conscious, unconscious, and uninformed choices that poor people make and that guide their individual behavior; she refers to this as "cognitive determinism." She believes if only they could learn how to make constructive decisions about how to act, they could escape from poverty. Her target is "generational poverty," which involves having been socialized dysfunctionally by poor parents and neighborhood peers. This is distinct from the random disasters that cause middle-class people to fall temporarily into "situational" poverty, from which they already know how to recover because they have been properly socialized. Generational poverty is like an inherited disease that can contaminate whole neighborhoods where poor people live, reproducing and spreading through social interaction and influence. In this scenario, larger issues of unemployment and discrimination are submerged and naturalized as simply the reality facing individuals born into poor families: "People in poverty face challenges virtually unknown to those in middle class or wealth—challenges from both obvious and hidden sources. The reality of being poor brings out a survival mentality, and turns attention away from opportunities taken for granted by everyone else."[6] The role of education, and related social policies, is to prepare children and adults to surmount those challenges and become productive citizens: "If you work with people in poverty, some understanding of how different their world is from yours will be invaluable. Whether you're an educator—or a social, health, or legal services professional—this breakthrough book gives you practical, real world support and guidance to improve your effectiveness in working with people from all socioeconomic backgrounds."[7] Payne's role is to provide middle-class professionals and volunteers with a clearer understanding of how to deal with poor people, and a set of tools that can be applied in tutoring them in how to be middle-class.

Framework is now in its fifth edition and has grossed somewhere between twenty-five and forty million dollars. With just under two hundred pages of text and ample white space, big type, and large graphics, it is highly readable and nonacademic by design. Her stated plan is to promote improved understanding across lines of social class, leading to increased mentorship by middle- and upper-class volunteers and guided self-improvement by those in the lower class. She refers to this idea as an "additive model" and has also used the term *economic pragmatism*. The basis for her claims is unconventional, coming almost entirely from her own thoughts, experience, and creative speculations. When she cites published research, her characterizations are often not in accord with the authors' own conclusions and interpretation. She has been criticized by a growing number of academic educational researchers, whose complaints she dismisses as the self-interested defensiveness of scholars who are more concerned about diversity than economics.[8] *Framework* is designed to be a users' manual, although it is not very specific about how the envisioned transformation will be effected. The format is a fairly breezy assortment of assertions illustrated by admittedly fictional vignettes. Participants are asked to assess these vignettes against matrices and checklists Payne has devised to illustrate her larger points about the dysfunctional culture of poor people. The book and supplementary materials are used in on-site lectures and workshops where teachers and other audiences are animated to join the fight against generational poverty. "For our students to be successful, we must understand their hidden rules and teach them rules that will make them successful at school and at work."[9]

One of the chapters, "The Role of Language and Story," describes the relationship between class and the use of linguistic "registers." Payne identifies five of these based on the work of linguist Martin Joos published in the 1960s. She claims that middle-class people know how to use the "formal" register, while poor people are mostly confined to use of the "casual" register, which stigmatizes them and inhibits their capacity to verbalize and find words to substitute for fists in arguments. Wayne O'Neill, a professor of linguistics at MIT with a specialty in educational linguistics (who studied under Joos), characterized her rendition of Joos's concepts as follows:

> Payne's discussion of language, in part modeled on Joos' five registers from his book *The Five Clocks*, is turned into a social-class based analysis (a strange three-level one—welfare, working class, professional class). Her idea is that class determines how large one's vocabulary is, how dense it is with abstract words, and so on. As far as I know, there is no research to support such notions. Class prejudice does, of course, support them, but that is prejudice, not science.[10]

Payne's advice is based on a faulty understanding of the science of linguistics. She appears to validate, incorrectly, a common belief about the cognitive limitations and language deficiencies of poor people. This is not a small shortcoming in a program designed to improve interclass communication and understanding.

A related goal is to close the social gap between the lower and middle classes. The importance of personal relationships is a key feature in Payne's vision, but it is a paradoxical message. Payne claims that poor people are mired in their personal relationships, the source of their bad upbringing and reinforcers of their wrong-headed ideas. Even if an individual manages to acquire a sum of money from a lottery ticket or some other fortuitous source, it will be squandered in helping kin and neighbors. For Payne, these relationships are a big part of the problem. "To move from poverty to middle class or middle class wealth, an individual must give up relationships for achievement (at least for some period of time)."[11] New relationships are needed, with people who can actually help, people who know other people who might have jobs to offer or other advantages. Quality social capital is built by creating "bridges" of understanding to sympathetic middle-class mentors who can guide poor people into a better life. Christian duty to help the poor is an implicit appeal, along with fiscal advantages of reducing poverty. Although she argues that poor people survive almost entirely on the basis of their family and neighborhood relationships (one of the hidden rules), to improve their condition as individuals they must shed these toxic bonds and form new ones with strangers who have been schooled by the program in reasons to look down on them.

Aha! I Get It Now

Payne's organization (aha! Process, Inc.) is a for-profit corporation headquartered in Highlands, Texas (a small city on the Gulf coast). All of her books are published in-house. Some have been reviewed in academic venues, but there is no peer review prior to publication and sale. The high volume of sales and relatively high prices for aha! books offer profitability not available to authors of academic books, who get only a small share of their publishers' proceeds. Payne founded the company in 1994, initially to produce and distribute *Framework*. The website of aha! Process, Inc. now has a rack with dozens of books, and a growing stable of authors and trainers of trainers. The website catalog has twenty-nine pages of products and services, along with brief testimonials and endorsements from satisfied customers. The inventory includes books, workbooks, DVDs, applications for iPad and Android devices, workshops, lectures, and training sessions. They even hawk coffee mugs, caps, and tee shirts.

There are four separate "Solutions" departments: K–12; higher education; communities; and individuals. In addition to schools, the corporation has cultivated relationships with law enforcement, community colleges and some colleges and universities, businesses, nonprofits, churches, philanthropists, and social services agencies. What began as a project to improve communication between middle-class teachers and low-income students has broadened into nearly all sectors of the so-called poverty industry. They train trainers in many locales, often including well-placed individuals in school districts, agencies, or other relevant organizations.[12] This approach is similar in some ways to those of Amway and other multilevel marketing strategies. Local insiders who stand to gain financially make good allies in securing contracts and finding new markets.

The community program is called "Bridges out of Poverty" and is based on systematic cultivation of elite and middle-class involvement in helping impoverished families and individuals learn new ways of thinking and behaving.[13] Poverty is too expensive for communities to afford; we all will benefit if we can resocialize troublesome poor people to work, pay taxes, and stay out of jail. Payne's slogan is to help build "sustainable communities where everyone can live well." Among the "foundational ideas" of the program is teaching the "four ways to get out of poverty: ownership of one's own *future story* [my emphasis], a good job, an education that leads to a good paying job, and bridging social capital."[14] The idea is to match middle-class poverty coaches with impoverished subjects who can be retrained to function in a middle-class world and be integrated into new more capital-laden social networks. The implementation strategy is a program titled "Getting Ahead in a Just Gettin'-By World." It promises instruction and aid to people "struggling to take charge" of their lives. Inductees are assigned mentors, who work with them individually. Support groups are also formed. Participants must agree to establish discipline and pledge to accept new values in exchange for assistance, which includes coaching, counseling, networking, and "life skills" training. Involvement with Bridges can also lead to help with housing, transportation, child care, and other critical material needs. These latter benefits make the programs irresistible, and who could argue with efforts to help deserving poor people find a path out of their condition? The math is difficult, however. There are massively more poor families than middle-class volunteers willing to take on the role of mentoring them. The website states that tens of thousands of people have been helped by the program. There is no documentation or specificity for this claim, but even if it is true, there are more than forty-six million poor people in the United States. Not all of them can find mentors.

The Bridges program has been deployed in a growing number of communities. Payne's principal collaborator is Philip DeVol, whose 2010 book cites many examples of places where trainers and facilitators have been hired. More have been added since publication. In some cities, the network of allied individuals and organizations is very dense. DeVol reports that at one time Syracuse, NY had a program with ninety Bridges trainers and sixteen Getting Ahead facilitators. In only a few years, there has been considerable expansion of Payne's system in Tampa, Florida where I live and work. I will describe some of that work shortly. However, I want to stop here first and consider the meaning of this very successful enterprise and, if it has no grounding in legitimate research-based knowledge about poverty, educational achievement, social capital, language registers, and related topics, and there is little evidence that it has had more than an anecdotal impact on poverty or poor people, then why has it been so phenomenally successful?

My own "aha" moment came when I watched a series of YouTube videos of Payne's lectures and appearances. She is an extremely talented performer. Her delivery and mode of narration is captivating and nondidactic. She weaves stories and homilies into an exhortation to rescue the unfortunate and serve the community. Based on her own scale of "language registers," hers veer between "casual" (poor people's diction) and "consultative" (middle-class conversational style). Although these are formal presentations, she does not rise to the "formal" register (where experts speak with precision). Her narration is folksy and meandering, and she spikes her stories with sensational or ludicrous, but highly memorable, images.

Payne's discussion of the culture of poverty is ostensibly sympathetic, and she also speaks of assets and "resources" that she claims people in poverty have. Their lives are a struggle and they make use of whatever they can. One can almost imagine her ending such a declaration with "bless their hearts." Indignant about claims that her work is racist and classist, she insists that she is color-blind, and that people of all races are poor and suffer from a shared set of bad habits. It is true that she does not address race directly, but racial stereotypes abound in her vignettes. Paul Gorski, a professor of education and critic of Payne, writes: "And although Payne ignores the relationship between poverty and racism, a review of her scenarios and case studies reveals that she does manage to incorporate a variety of racist stereotypes into her framework. Not only does Payne (2005) name the racial identities of each of her families in the scenarios (and why do this if she intends to focus solely on class?), but she also paints glaringly racist portraits of her African American and Latino characters."[15]

For example, "Otis is a 9-year-old African-American boy. His mother conceived him at 14, dropped out of school, and is on welfare. Otis has two younger siblings and *one* older sibling who is a gang member."[16] As the scenario unfolds, we learn that Otis's mother, twenty-four years old, has had five children, the first when she was only thirteen. She currently has an abusive boyfriend who is in jail. She is behind on her rent and the family is going to have to move, again. Otis's teacher called her to say he was misbehaving at school. His mother beat him with a belt, and then forgave him, but never told him to change his behavior at school. Rules are different if you are poor. Teachers need to know they might trigger violence, or at least will not get the predicted result from normal contact with poor parents. The lesson here was supposed to have been the part about harsh discipline without appropriate sanctions or feedback, but the takeaway was a broader reinforcement of existing negative stereotypes about poor black mothers and their children. Each scenario contains such a dual lesson, and all of them woven together form the corpus of her data and an assortment of the hidden rules. Recall that these are all imaginary poor people whom Payne has deliberately wrapped in the insignia of race and gender, along with class. Gorski points out that "Payne identifies violent tendencies, whether in the form of gang violence or child abuse in three of the four families of color . . . but not in any of the three white families. Each of the families of color, but only one of the three white families, features at least one unemployed or sporadically employed working-age adult. Whereas two of the three white children have at least one stable caretaker, three of the four children of color . . . appear to have none."[17]

If not racist, these vignettes are at least pejorative, which is their intent. They are designed to be shocking and to set forth a stark contrast with the experiences and values of her reader or audience. Sex and violence are a prominent part of the narrative, especially among the black and Latino families described. Like Moynihan, Harrington, and Lewis, Payne appears to be using sensationalism to arouse sympathy in her audiences. This approach also is a successful strategy for engaging public attention, but as discussed earlier, it seems more effective at evoking conservative beliefs and punitive impulses.

As a translator of research and clinical knowledge, Payne is not credible; her sources are frequently inappropriate, incorrectly cited, or lacking altogether. Many of her assertions are naive. A thirty-year marriage does not qualify as a "longitudinal study." Fabricated vignettes are not data. And there is scant reliable evidence that her interventions produce any measures of success. What she is really accomplished at, however, is marketing. She has developed a corporate powerhouse in the poverty industry, and the product she is vending resonates extremely well with neoliberal thinking about both poverty and the appropriate solutions for fixing it. Her well-crafted message appeals to conservative funders and elected officials, and to middle-class professionals struggling to do more with less and facing worsening poverty issues in their work. Those faith-based charities most known for judgmental tendencies also respond well to the Bridges appeal.

The resulting programs are infused with paternalism and a conviction that most poor people share a culture that has damaged their capacity to reason and control their impulses. Relationships created in this kind of tutorial arrangement are inherently unequal, patronizing, and likely to be tense. The notion of "maximum feasible participation" has completely disappeared. The Bridges approach, and Payne's whole system, is the political opposite of what was originally planned in the OEO a half century ago. Poor people are not partners in this effort. They are the problem; their condition disqualifies their opinions. The mission is to rescue individuals willing to undergo transformation. As the price of success they are supposed to sever connections to their families and friends. Demobilization and atomization (i.e., dispersal and individualism) appear to be among the desired outcomes.

Bridges to Tampa

For the past several years, the Payne system has been operating in Tampa, Florida in various sites and to varied degrees. Her company had a string of contracts funded by Title I federal grants for years with the Hillsborough County School District, eighth largest in the United States. When I first became aware of her involvement in the schools, in about 2009, local opposition was emerging among some parents and community activists, but there was strong support for Payne within the administration and among a majority of the school board members. Early on I attended a small public meeting that had been requested by a retired educator who had taken on the project of opposing the use of Payne's program in Tampa's schools. Present was the district's Title I coordinator, a strong supporter of Payne, and a number of parents she seemed to know personally. Testimonials proffered in that meeting appeared to confirm that there was strong support among teachers and parents, and the instigator of the meeting was somewhat rudely dismissed in statements by the Title I coordinator. A few months later, however, another public meeting was held on this topic, this time sponsored by the education committee of a community center in an African American neighborhood. In this venue, the tenor of the audience was very different. For a Saturday morning it was a fairly large gathering, about fifty people. The retired educator turned community activist gave a formal presentation explaining *Framework* and outlining criticisms of the claims and objections to the pejorative nature of the content. Present in the audience was the president of the school board, who spoke against further use of the system in the county schools. She had grown up in a working-class Latino family and found the vignettes offensive. Unlike before, few in this meeting defended Payne. Several parents offered stories with complaints. An education professor stated that Payne's system demeans children and their parents and is counterproductive training for teachers. Toward the back of the room was a small group of people who appeared to be together. During the audience participation, a man in the group stood and identified himself as one of Payne's consultants. He defended her program and disputed the criticism.

Within a week of the meeting, Payne herself penned a two-page letter to the superintendent of the district complaining about the criticism that had been aired. She offered the following: "The meeting appeared to target my work because of a fear within university departments and some community members that economic diversity issues will undermine racial diversity issues. Apparently, my work related to economic issues has become a lightning rod for individuals who are seeking election, reelection, or public attention."[18] The letter references "your staff members who have become certified trainers," suggesting they can be helpful in clearing up any misunderstanding.

This rapid response, condemning her critics as professionally jealous defenders of turf, is a clumsy but predictable tactic. Part of the corporate model is to crush competition and silence criticism. Gorski recounts his experiences with her response machine. Her lawyer had contacted him after he gave a presentation at a national conference.

"Cease and desist," the attorney warned during our phone conversation, "or Ms. Payne will sue." Her attorney also called the hosting organization, insisting that its board of directors do a better job of monitoring the content and titles of presentations. Although I never heard from her attorney again, I did hear from one of the central members of her consulting team—a man who once worked for the university where I am employed . . . he proceeded to seek assistance from several of my more senior colleagues. When they would not comply he complained to the director of my academic department, then my dean, and continued straight up the power structure all the way to president of the university. No luck. Finally, in perhaps the ultimate act of anti-intellectualism, he began calling organizations that had invited me to speak or consult, trying to convince them to un-invite me.[19]

The reportedly uncollegial treatment of Gorski reflects both the seriousness of the business and a manipulative and punitive dimension present in the program philosophy itself.

The Hillsborough County School District apparently decided not to renew the contract with Payne in 2013, according to a different school board member who attended a later public meeting also called to complain about Payne. In the meantime, however, a consortium of local charities and philanthropies had joined to bring Payne to Tampa to institute Bridges and Getting Ahead programs.[20] The Tampa Junior League was a principal partner in the arrangement, along with several major local poverty-serving agencies and the United Way. The Bank of America and the Tampa Bay Rays baseball team owner were major corporate supporters. Sacrifice, discipline, and fidelity are regarded as critical traits for escaping from poverty in the Bridges program. Tough love and autocracy are deemed to be necessary ingredients. One of the early facilitators of this expansion is director of a local program that followed Payne's basic formula, called Starting Right, Now (SRN). The main focus of this program is rescuing homeless teens and helping them make the transition into a functioning adulthood. Offering a laudable goal and much-needed service, they work with the kinds of families who appear in Payne's scenarios—families with dad in jail and mom a hopeless addict, where older kids are likely to end up on the streets. Such families and teens do exist in too large numbers in Tampa and most other cities. SRN's website describes their purpose and method: "We intercede at a critical juncture in a child's life, breaking the generational cycle of poverty. Unlike other agencies, we provide a deep, holistic and personal approach to end homelessness one family, one child, at a time. We are not a hand-out, we are not a band-aid. We cure homelessness, achieving remarkable results. STARTING RIGHT, NOW is ending homelessness, one child at a time."[21]

SRN is kind of like boot camp. No indulgence, no excuses. The teens are presumed to be unsocialized and without proper values or discipline, in need of a stern hand and a careful watchful eye. Teens accepted into the program are assigned jobs for twenty hours a week and have to attend school every day. According to press reports, they are provided with housing and are assigned personal mentors who have keys to their apartments and access to their phones, email, and online bank accounts. Mentors can enter their apartments at any time without notice. Participants must follow strict guidelines and sign a contract agreeing to abide by all of the rules.[22] The program can support up to twenty-four clients at a time. One child at a time, or even twenty-four, is a very slow pace, especially given the large increase in the homeless teen population since the foreclosure and jobs crisis of 2008 (SRN was founded in 2007). However, the stories about their struggles and victories are genuinely inspiring. The website contains several of these accounts; SRN claims to have helped more than one hundred kids with a success rate of 90 percent.

SRN has been extremely successful in fund-raising and winning awards for its achievements. The Board of Directors includes the mayor of Tampa, the superintendent of schools, and the owner of the Tampa Bay Rays. They have attracted large sums in donations and volunteer commitments, and have garnered a great deal of positive press coverage. In the summer of 2013, however, they attracted some unwanted publicity when a story broke about two homeless teens who were being sued for many thousands of dollars for violating their SRN contracts. According to the *Tampa Bay Times,* "Starting Right, Now has twice sued teens who left the non-profit's exacting program. The charity asserts the young women are liable for money it spent on expenses such as food, rent, electricity, clothing, and—in one case—a Christmas Tree."

One of the defendants in the suit was unaware that a judgment had been obtained that she owed the charity $18,245. The other, whose judgment was smaller but still quite a lot ($3,006), had been aware of the action against her but, without a lawyer, had agreed to a repayment plan. The director of SRN explained: "Before anyone is removed from our program, he or she is provided many opportunities to change behavior and comply with our guidelines. If that does not occur, we remove the student from the program and seek repossession of donated property and repayment of services, as is stipulated in the agreement (signed by participants.) . . . We take legal action only as a last resort, and we do so to preserve the integrity of our program and to conserve resources for current and future students."[23]

The value of these two as examples to the other participants might also be part of the logic. One of the sued teens said, "I was trying so hard to not go back to the way I was, but after this, it made it so much worse." These particular cases did not work out well, which is understandable in such a difficult program. And it is quite believable that the other teens, those who have been successful, are fully grateful and on their way to having happier lives. The treatment of the two young women, however, aroused a lot controversy and criticism. Discipline is one thing, but putting homeless teenagers into heavy adult debt because they were unable to complete an admittedly harsh program seemed to many to be over the top. It turned out the agreements they had signed as minors were not legally enforceable.

SRN soon announced a change in its policy of taking wayward participants to court, and they have continued to operate their program in prosperous respectability. A recent news story about them had a much happier result.[24] A young homeless teen struggling to finish high school was rescued by SRN. She had the dad in jail/bad mother combination, and had left home to find a different way. She studied hard, joined the track team at her high school, got a part-time job from 5 to 11 p.m. on weekdays, kept her clothes in the trunk of the car she managed to buy (where she slept each night), and showered at school. She did all of this on her own. Weary and afraid she might not make it to graduation, she told a counselor who connected her with SRN. They were able to provide exactly what she needed: a safe place to stay and study and help getting a track scholarship to a local college. Truly an uplifting story, and very fortunate that they were able to reach her. However, this is not a young woman who needed lessons in discipline, or managing money, or making the right choices. She received invaluable assistance that can make a huge difference in her future, but she was required to submit to needless tutelage and humiliating oversight in exchange for that benefit. This girl's story is one of a handful of examples that have been portrayed in local human interest stories. Several adults who have participated in Payne's *Getting Ahead* programs offered by the Salvation Army and other local agencies also have been the subjects of coverage. Most were thrown into poverty and homelessness through the loss of a job.

A lot of that was happening, and a lot of people were and still are losing their homes, which is one way to become homeless. Some of the featured subjects had advanced degrees and no sign of any pathology, except being laid off and broke.[25] They got help, and were experiencing success (the reason for the coverage), but like the above teen in SRN they were required to undergo what appear to have been needless and insulting tutorial programs and surrender significant control.

Payne's critics do not deny that some families are irretrievably broken, and that some kids have a critical need for structure and discipline that has not existed in their lives. Familial pathology that prevents kids from learning or maturing constructively does occur, as do all sorts of human pathologies that should be treated in a well-functioning society. Low-income individuals who lack the resources to obtain treatment should be identified and assisted. This group, however, is reckoned to be a small minority among the many low-income people whose kids are struggling in school, or who might themselves fall into distress and need help. The harsh and patronizing elements of the program are not necessary, justifiable, or appropriate in most cases; they perpetuate the belief that people in poverty lack good judgment, and reinforce those hidden rules that maintain power in interclass relationships.

Mick Arran, a self-described radical education blogger, offered the following cynical but interesting analysis of why he thinks Payne has been such a successful marketer:

> If you are a business, you cannot afford to sell yourself on the basis of individualized services: you'd have to charge way more than you could expect any financially-strapped school to be able to pay. So you don't. You do what Payne did and concentrate on the LCD [lowest common denominator], selling your service as something applicable to the dominant pool [all poor people]. In order to do that, you then have to develop stereotypes that fit your supposed model and try to convince your customers that their clients mostly fit neatly into it and will be helped by it. Since it does fit a healthy 15% of the total client pool, the customers will, in fact, see some improvement.[26]

The poster successes of SRN and Getting Ahead fit this assessment. The ones who make it prove it works, but many who make it are likely those, like the teen track star, who needed it least from the standpoint of behavioral and attitudinal reform. They play along so they don't lose the needed benefits that are available. Others, who actually do fit the stereotype, may be the ones who wash out of the program. But what is the harm if it helps some of the participants, even if more sternly than needed? Our blogger has an answer: "Unfortunately, it *can* have a lasting negative effect. What happens is that the stereotypes developed by a businesswoman like Payne for sale to schools [and community organizations] become a sort of template ever after in which the signs and techniques ... [that are] bought from her become short-hand markers that will tend to label kids [and adults] in a certain way and result in a treatment modality utterly unsuited for their actual condition."

Ruby Payne is not the only source of programs for schools and communities struggling with poverty. She is, however, arguably the most successful in terms of both revenue and reach. Many other private consultants and government-sponsored programs are intended to reach struggling students, their families, and young adults. Most are variants of the same culture of poverty orientation, like SRN, including a great many of the local agencies in Tampa that we have worked with over the years. A guiding principle that nearly all have shared is the conviction that poor people need to be molded and remediated, to transform themselves to be able to join in the prosperity of the larger society. Unspoken in this presumption is how rarely that actually works, especially when the tide of newly poor keeps rapidly expanding. Also unstated is how this perspective completely neglects the external causes of poverty. This view also does not take sufficient account of the varied reasons that people find themselves in this predicament. For instance, a young woman with an MA who was laid off from a professional job in the recession exhausted her savings, had no family to fall back on, and became homeless. Someone in that predicament needs help, but she does not need lessons, or discipline, or to be made to feel like she is a failure. (Actually, there is no justification for deliberately making any struggling individuals feel worse about themselves.) As Arran suggests, the real costs of this approach to combating poverty are the needless humiliation of the recipients and the reinforcement of stereotypes about class, race, and gender. Alternative programs, like those developed by Lisa Delpit, flip this script; her approach is that poor black kids need to learn how to code switch (i.e., speak and dress like middle-class white kids) when the need arises for their own self-preservation, but they also need to know why such dissembling is necessary and to learn the history of African American struggle.[27] Although arguably more successful in motivating and energizing young black students, her message and purpose sells less well. When schools and agencies are in a panic about control, they are likely less willing to risk arousing anger over truthful renditions of the problems they confront.

The focus of this discussion should not be about Ruby Payne or any other individual poverty entrepreneur. Like the Moynihan Report itself, Ruby is the embodiment of a trope, a tangible image for framing discussion. Her meteoric rise and the clever marketing and packaging she has developed are the point—her calculated use of well-worn stereotypes that seem to resonate so successfully. She serves as an especially apt example of how Moynihan's ideas about family structure and Lewis's writing about the culture of the poor have evolved over the decades into the faux compassionate face of neoliberalism. There are still grassroots programs, like Obadiah, and others less beleaguered, that have held to the premise of what anthropologist Ward Goodenough long ago described as "cooperation in change" and that adhere to the same logic as the "guerillas in the Office of Economic Opportunity who believed that community organizing was the best way to fight poverty."[28] In the next and final chapter, I will return to this contrast between therapeutic and community organizing approaches, revisit the concept of collective efficacy, and argue the need to expand cultural analyses beyond the alleged traits and values of the poor to focus more squarely on the persistent racism and venomous greed that pervades the behavior and values of those who actually rule our society.

7

Ending Poverty as
We Know It

• • • • • • • • • • • • • • • • • •

And Other Apparently
Unreachable Goals

> The asymmetry of power can indeed generate
> a kind of quiet brutality. We know, of course,
> that power corrupts and absolute power cor-
> rupts absolutely. But inequalities of power in
> general prevent the sharing of different oppor-
> tunities. They can devastate the lives of those
> who are far removed from the levers of control.
> —Amartya Sen, quoted in Paul Farmer, *The*
> *Pathologies of Power*

In the foregoing chapters, I have tried to peel back the layers of disingenuous, distanced, and delusional beliefs that lead otherwise sensible people to
think that poverty in the United States is principally caused by poor people
themselves, by their inabilities to compete in school or the workplace, and
their unrestrained impulses and violent tendencies. This viewpoint implies

that the invisible hand of the market has sorted the lesser among us into a lower rung of society where disadvantages of inherent lack of ability or ambition in one generation may be passed to the next in an unfortunate cycle of inherited failure reinforced by life in an environment of multiple risks. From the eugenics enthusiasts of the early twentieth century (which included an embarrassing number of social liberals) to outwardly sympathetic reformers in the current era like Ruby Payne, and eminent researchers like William J. Wilson, Douglas Massey, and Robert Sampson who proudly declare their liberal *bona fides*, the implication that poor people are incapable of or not ready for "maximum feasible participation," or any real say in decisions that affect their lives and futures, reflects a set of assumptions that conform rather directly to the tangle of pathology meme.

Moynihan did not invent this idea; indeed it can be traced to the Middle Ages, and possibly back to the initial emergence of landed property and the power to force others to work against their interests. To disparage those you are exploiting is an obvious ploy with timeless appeal. Moynihan's contribution to the more recent longevity of this meme was in many ways fortuitous. Consider the many thousands of government reports that have moldered on shelves and in boxes never to see the light of day, never to have any impact. I have submitted a few of these myself in summations of the National Science Foundation (NSF) grant research on HOPE VI and other funded projects designed to produce social science knowledge. So why Moynihan's? It was not very well designed, executed, or written. It got a decidedly mixed reception, ranging from enthusiastic endorsements to scorching criticism. A large number of respected scholars quickly disputed and disabused the main findings and conclusions.

It Is Hard to Kill a Bad Idea That Serves the Powerful

In an interesting footnote to the earlier story about Carol Stack's breakfast with Oscar and Pat, in her address at the Twenty-Fifth Anniversary Conference of *All Our Kin*, she related the following:

> Watching the two of them nodding heads in agreement, and seeing how Lewis's findings had reached the eyes and ears of a person working for the Johnson administration was amazing. Research, I whispered to myself, can make a difference. It was only years later, when I had something to say, and worked along

with welfare rights organizations against social policies that had terrible consequences for people they might have been designed to help, that I stumbled on a *very hard lesson*. What I took away from that breakfast was that scholars can have an impact on social policy, if the policy makers and those in power share the same perspectives.[1]

Those in power tend to like the kind of ideas and remedies that Ruby Payne is prescribing, despite the lack of a rigorous evidential basis. There is also widespread support for the entirely rigorous and academically respectable research on the effects of concentrated poverty and potential benefits of deconcentration, even though there is scant evidence that relocating poor people from one low-resourced neighborhood to another (which is how it turned out for the most part) has produced benefits remotely commensurate with the costs (both to taxpayers and relocatees). And despite substantial evidence that ties marriage rates to the economy, and declines in marriage to a deteriorating labor market, most pundits and many researchers continue to argue that a simple cure for poverty is more marriage and delayed child bearing. Poor people need to learn how to control their sexual and emotional impulses and be more like the middle class.

The shaming and humiliation of people in poverty are examples of what Paul Farmer and others have labeled "structural violence." A concept adopted from Johan Galtung, the liberation theologian who coined it in 1969, Farmer uses this term: "[A]s a broad rubric that includes a host of offenses against human dignity: extreme and relative poverty, social inequalities ranging from racism to gender inequality, and the more spectacular forms of violence that are uncontestedly human rights abuses, some of them punishments for efforts to escape structural violence."[2] The pejorative and demeaning images of poverty, patronizing and judgmental treatment by many charities and public agencies, and the punitive hand of the carceral state (which shows itself as early as preschool) are all examples of structural violence. The penalties of birth into a low-income family, especially one that is black or Latino, include personal experiences with most or all of these. The popular narrative misleadingly ascribes this structural disadvantage to an absence of books in the homes of poor parents who don't read to their children, or give them the moral values needed to withstand the temptations of adolescence. The material capacity to provide kids with space to study and resources needed to do their school work, and the wherewithal to live in a neighborhood with decent schools, and confidence that completing high school will lead to college and a satisfying adulthood: those are the real components of success for children in the middle class and the essential features that few poor families can provide regardless of how virtuous or committed they are to their children.

Even if some of the bright and ambitious can be located and saved by enlightened philanthropists, the vast majority remain unnoticed and unassisted. Moreover, the tough love of Starting Right, Now and similar programs that extend conditional lifesavers to individuals who are drowning, may be intended to build discipline and confidence, but the philosophy and medium of delivery demand strict obedience that can engender resentment and reinforce negative stereotypes and unequal relations. And it can be argued that these rescues have done more to advance the rescuers than the project of eliminating poverty. Wealthy philanthropists and middle-class professionals can bask in the storied accomplishments of a handful of their charges. Corporate scoundrels, such as the banks that engineered the mortgage foreclosure scams that inflicted a lot more poverty on the already struggling neighborhood where we work in Tampa, and devastated the formerly middle-class foreclosure victims we interviewed in our study of the Tampa Bay area, are celebrated for their measly charitable contributions and very public support for the hard work of saving the poor—one child at a time.[3]

Times They Were A-changin', But Not in a Good Way

For the forces of revanchism in the 1960s, Moynihan was the right guy with the right idea when our nation was headed for an abrupt right turn. Moynihan's role was relatively minor. He did not orchestrate the urban disturbances of the summers of 1964 and 1965; he did not sabotage the Community Action Programs that were somewhat independently flaming out in the same period; and he did nothing to bring on the disastrous war in Vietnam and the unruly demonstrations by throngs of college kids and others who were refusing to fight in it. What he did do was deliver a succinct and timely narrative that served actors in the conservative response extremely well. He was part of what Steve Steinberg has called "the left wing of the backlash."[4] In his treatise on the rise of the carceral state, Loic Wacquant refers to Moynihan as one of "the chief ideologues of American political reaction."[5] He is one of only three whom Wacquant mentioned in this context, along with Charles Murray and conservative political scientist Lawrence Mead. It is an association that Moynihan likely would have hotly disputed, although he was known to keep company with neoconservatives like James Q. Wilson and Irving Kristol.

Through a long career in public life, Moynihan proved to be a highly complex and self-contradictory figure. An avowed liberal, he seems to have been genuinely shaken and appalled by the unrest of the 1960s and firm in his belief that the dangers it posed to society were coming from below. Writing in 1987 about the recent past and coming future, he reiterated his earlier arguments about the perils of single parenthood. But he also focused on the growing unfairness in the economy and its effects on children and families: "I have come to think of this as The Great Divide. In a space of a few years in the late sixties and early seventies, the incomparable growth in American society that began in World War II came to an end. During that period of growth, family income grew as if by some physical law. Never once did three years go by without a new record being broken. Now it all stopped."[6] In this epilogue to his book, *Family and Nation*, which followed up on the 1965 report, Moynihan weighed the impacts of the policies and politics he had come to know as a senator.[7] He excoriated the Reagan administration for gutting social spending and declaring war on the public sector. He presented well chosen data that clearly confirmed downward trends in wealth and opportunity for a growing share of US families. He saw the systemic nature of the problem he had wrestled with, but he did not follow up on that key insight. Instead, he returned to family structure and what he viewed as the "pathology of industrial society." His own data beg questions he either failed to notice or was unwilling to answer.

In his later musing about the "Sixties Scissors," Moynihan implied that this seismic shift was a regrettable corrective for the excesses of protest and radical ideas about family and liberation. Perhaps he was too willing to see the metaphorical hand of God in the social pain that emerged, rather than recognize the human hands that were working to create these conditions. Beginning long before the 1960s, and especially during the depression of the 1930s, self-appointed captains of industry and finance have been (and still are) waging a relentless campaign against both organized labor and public expenditures that benefit poor people. They have deployed considerable resources into political organizations (like the John Birch Society and more recently Americans for Prosperity). And they developed a multitude of foundations and think tanks (e.g., The Heritage Foundation, Cato

Institute, etc.), which better enable them to influence public opinion and steer enactment of laws and regulations. Propaganda efforts to roll back progressive changes in government and society were aided immeasurably by the upheavals and violence of the late 1960s. Fearful slogans and images stirred opposition, especially among white working-class voters. The reach of these extremely wealthy activists is more extensive and powerful today than it was then, exemplified in the American Legislative Exchange Council (ALEC), a nonprofit organization where laws against collective bargaining, in favor of punitive sentencing, and in support of many other reactionary projects have been crafted and handed off to willing legislators.

Engineers of the "culture wars" had a lot to work with in the late 1960s. At that time several wars were going on, against crime, drugs, the counter-culture, angry black people, angry women, and grandest of all, the real war in Vietnam. I graduated from college in 1968. I remember that year as one of horror and demoralization, political assassinations, urban uprisings, and the shocking Democratic convention when the war came home to Grant Park and the streets of Chicago, and Mayor Daley was caught on TV cursing at Senator Abraham Rubicoff with "fuck you, you Jew son of a bitch" for condemning what later came to be called a "police riot."[8] Unsettled times to be sure, and far from over. The "days of rage" that followed were really months of rage, and the Weather Underground became the terrorists *du jour*, along with the Black Panthers. I vividly recall the weekend when the Weather People trashed Harvard Square in Cambridge. Although not sympathetic with their actions, I remember going there the next day, perversely curious to see if the mostly glass building of Design Research, symbol of vapid elite consumerism, had suffered much damage (it hadn't). For a great many opponents of the war and supporters of social equality, including myself, these were indeed ambivalent and worrisome times.

By many accounts, we reached more than a cultural turning point in that spring and summer of 1968; it was also the beginning of what Moynihan and others have labeled the "Great Divide." Virtually all the graphs that depict growing inequality and declining wages take off shortly thereafter. The trend lines that show strong associations among factors like increased wealth at the very top, declining household incomes, and plummeting union membership seem highly inconsistent with the idea that poverty comes from the bad behavior of poor people. Over the decades since the end of the 1960s (when poverty had sunk nearly to the lowest point ever), poverty rates can be seen to spike during recessions and fall during periods of increased employment. All these covariant data support structural arguments, a reflection of elite forces within the national and global economy, and the political influence they wield over the distribution of opportunities on the ground. But, as already discussed at length, data and evidence about poverty are highly contested.

The Epistemology of Poverty

A major concern in this book has been exploring the basis of what historian Alice O'Connor calls "poverty knowledge." How do we know, or think we know, what poverty is and, more important, what are its causes? In chapter 2, I attempted to review and consider this body of research and writing, with a focus on how ideas spawned by the culture of poverty and the tangle of pathology viewpoints have influenced perceptions and convictions about poor people. Poverty research is not like physics. Definitive research designs, experiments that lay bare the chain of causation, are not very feasible. Problems besetting the Moving to Opportunity quasi-experiment described in chapter 4 illustrate the vicissitudes of trying to exercise control and devise adequate measurements of actually occurring social interventions.

A divide exists between researchers who rely primarily on large data sets and quantitative analyses, on one side, and those who engage in intimate ethnographies in relatively small places, on the other. Many researchers, including myself, use mixed methods that combine quantitative data with qualitative interviews and participant observation. Numbers can be misleading and interview respondents sometimes lie; efforts to check one against the other can be profitable. More substantively, close acquaintance with people who suffer from the condition one is trying to understand, offers a relevant perspective if only for the sake of validity. Such an approach can generate better-informed hypotheses to define and guide the collection of quantitative data. That combination, however, still does not solve the larger question of how to study such a loaded concept as poverty. Although ethnographers tend to be more sympathetic to the external pressures on poor families and the effects of structural forces on their lives, this is not uniformly the case or necessarily the most important distinction. Ethnographers bring their own perspectives into the field and see and interpret events and circumstances in ways that a different observer might not, as with Oscar Lewis versus Charles Valentine or Eleanor Leacock. Quantitative researchers choose their own questions and may overinterpret results that are equivocal or amenable to alternative opinions, as in the implicit causality of neighborhood effects on poverty—the notion that living in a disadvantaged neighborhood is an independent cause of poverty, apart from the obvious fact that poverty and race determine where poor people can live—agglomerating their problems for statistical purposes in places that are underserved and overpoliced. Moynihan thought he had the key to the difference in his "scissors" measure, a mistaken belief that is still repeated as if it were fact. Whatever the relative merits and drawbacks of the different ways poverty has been studied, it is undeniably the case that quantitative results get more attention in policy circles, especially when (as Stack suggested) the findings point in acceptable directions.

Culture versus Structure

An important theoretical and policy distinction resides in the long-standing conflict about whether, or to what extent, structural or cultural forces are responsible for such high levels of poverty in the most affluent society in the history of the world. Structural factors include labor market conditions and economic and social policies that affect access to needed services and opportunities. Cultural issues affecting poverty are conventionally framed as habits and value orientations that poor people learn in childhood and from the differential associations of low-income people living in neighborhoods of "concentrated disadvantage." I have argued that limiting the analysis to the distinctive cultural practices of poor people ignores powerful cultural influences that emanate from above. Mounting evidence indicates that if there is a parallel condition that might be called the "culture of wealth," it reflects smug, stingy attitudes, selfish and uncaring values, and antisocial behaviors that can cause damage to the whole society, especially to those who are poor. I am not suggesting that all wealthy people exhibit such characteristics, which would entail a different form of statistical discrimination, but such generalizations are no less valid than the narrative contained in the culture of poverty thesis. Culture, as we faithfully teach in introductory anthropology courses, is holistic. It is systemic and interdependent. We need to interrogate the whole; studying poverty culture without cognizance of the cultural beliefs and motives of those who produce the inequality that leads to poverty is misleading. Ultimately it is a disservice to those who suffer and to a broader understanding of conditions we all experience.

Few proponents of either the cultural or structural approach claim that poverty stems from only one of these sources. Moynihan and W. J. Wilson are both on record repeatedly stating the importance of unemployment and discrimination, as well as the behavioral and attitudinal barriers that poor people themselves allegedly erect, in the persistence of poverty among the urban "underclass." In the past decade a large number of sociologists have turned to culture in an effort to understand vexing social phenomena like poverty. In 2010 the *Annals of the American Academy of Political and Social Science* published a special issue devoted to the topic "Reconsidering Culture and Poverty." The articles cover a variety of poverty-related concerns, illustrating the value of "meaning-making" in discerning patterns of behavior and professed values that can be elicited from people in poverty, giving insight into how they are or are not coping with their condition. The editors of the issue introduce the subject in this way: "Culture is back on the poverty research agenda. Over the past decade, sociologists, demographers, and even economists have begun asking questions about the role of culture in many aspects of poverty and even explicitly explaining the behavior of the low income population in reference to cultural factors."[9]

In response to this "cultural turn," Stephen Steinberg and Herbert Gans published separate dissenting articles.[10] Both take issue with the efficacy of the approach and the political implications of this focus. Responding to articles about research that elicited concepts of a "good job" or "infidelity" among low-income African American men, Steinberg asks: "Does it really matter how they define a 'good job' when they have virtually no prospect of finding one? Does it matter how they approach procreation, how they juggle 'doubt, duty, and destiny' when they are denied the jobs that are the *sine qua non* of parenthood? Aren't we asking the wrong questions?" Gans is similarly critical of searching for answers to questions that don't have much relevance for finding ways to solve problems related to poverty: "From my perspective, focusing on how poor people think and feel is not the most important subject for policy-oriented research on poverty. . . . The poor lack political power, and the holders of economic and political power are not particularly interested in reducing or eliminating poverty. Consequently, antipoverty agencies must deal with more urgent issues than worry about how the ostensible beneficiaries and other targets of their policies feel."[11]

From my experience Gans is correct that in policy circles there is scant interest in how poor people feel. The emphasis on culture, however, has strongly influenced the nature and goals of poverty programs, especially compared with ideas about how to change oppressive structures that are so active in the lives of low-income families. Cultural remediation approaches to ending poverty—e.g., Bridges out of Poverty, Starting Right, Now, and marriage promotion programs—will always win this contest for reasons of political expediency, and they will never actually work for reasons hopefully made clear in the preceding chapters. Viewing both culture and structure as equally implicated is an insufficient and ultimately misleading compromise. The tandem rise in inequality and poverty, the steadily declining wage-to-productivity ratio, globalization and outsourcing, and the capture of politics by big money corporate interests are the underlying factors that depress family incomes and thwart opportunities for young adults, whether they drop out of high school or manage to finish college under a crushing burden of debt. Fixing up individuals who need more self-esteem and better role models will never solve or even address those larger problems. This is not to suggest that mentoring or casework with individuals in need of help, or classes that help inexperienced parents to learn important facts about babies and children, and each other, should be abolished. These are the essential palliatives that we should provide more of, and that should be conducted with more respect and empathy for the participants than is frequently accorded. But these are band-aids on a putrefying wound. Without reforming distorted structures of banking, real estate, criminal justice, public education, and civic participation these measures will not stanch the tide of poverty. Without addressing joblessness and inadequate wages, the real root cause of poverty, there is no hope of real progress.

Racism and Culture

Racism is cultural. It is learned, shared, and acts as an implicit (sometimes explicit) social boundary–protecting mechanism. It is socially constructed and strategically inculcated and deployed. The vicious stereotypes that purport to explain and define poor people, especially those who are not white, are likewise cultural phenomena. The ubiquity of stereotyping and scapegoating in human history perhaps makes these practices seem natural and inevitable. It is possible to do a functional analysis of why these distortions work the way they do, and why they provide rulers with attractive control devices in highly unequal multiethnic societies, but so does female genital mutilation serve obvious purposes in societies where women are cloistered. Anthropologists a long time ago got over the notion that cultural relativism condones such practices, and we know that culture can/does change.

Economists have argued that "statistical racism" is rational behavior. Decision makers need heuristics; common knowledge about job seekers of varied ethnicity (i.e., stereotypes) may be the only clues available to those who hire low-skilled workers. What else can they do but discriminate against those who come from groups reputed to be unreliable and possibly dangerous? By a ratio of two to one, they hire white applicants and reject the equally qualified minorities. How rational is it to exclude perfectly well qualified applicants over those from favored groups, who actually may be less able individuals who will prove to be unreliable and maybe even dangerous? Artificially narrowing the pool of otherwise suitable choices would seem to increase the chances of making an incorrect hire, not lessen them. In many cases individual white workers are not satisfactory and individual black workers prove to be highly effective. However, based on Pager and Karafin's findings discussed in chapter 3, such stereotype-defying experiences apparently have negligible impact on employer attitudes about race. With such a large supply of surplus labor, maybe such lessons do not matter to bosses. Of course, they do matter to the large number of jobless African American men whose failure to marry the mothers of their children is cause for condemnation.

Opponents of the abolition of slavery argued that their position was rational also, that Africans were biologically unsuited to be free laborers in the South. Their case rested on biological racism, since discredited. The case for statistical racism rests on assumptions about culture. The employers quoted in Pager and Karafin's article offered the following: "They don't want to work—you can tell by the attitude, clothing, the general body language." "Just being lazy and not wanting to work." "Maybe they think that this country owes them so much. Because of slavery and all that . . . feel like they deserve something . . . [so] they don't want to work." "A lot of these people just don't have any work values." The references are cultural, but the thinking revealed in this outcropping of employer beliefs is nakedly racist. In the United States that is a cultural problem of too many white people (especially but not exclusively) that deserves to be identified as such and, in the case of those who hold power over others, should be vigorously attacked in policy and law. Cultural sociologists (and anthropologists) should take up that problem, and identify the "scripts" and "meaning-making" that drive the decisions of employers, police, public officials, corporations, financiers, and other sectors wherein racial biases contribute to poverty.

Social Engineering or Community Development

The programs described in chapters 3, 4, and 6—marriage promotion, deconcentration, and guided self-improvement—fall loosely into the category of social engineering. Experts design programmatic solutions to problems that are the subject of empirical research, based on what those studies seem to indicate is needed to alter a major social problem, poverty in this case. The data indicate that unmarried parenting is closely associated with poverty; *ergo* promoting marriage should help ease that problem. Concentrated poverty is associated with a long litany of social ills; relocate residents out of high-poverty areas and they should do better. Class barriers are preventing teachers, agency staff, and many volunteers from working effectively with low-income children and families; make them more sympathetic by explaining how culturally deviant these families are. These are the rationales for the programs described in this book, efforts ostensibly designed to ameliorate poverty and reengineer the behavioral and cultural factors that research has indicated may be responsible for the impoverished conditions of such a large number of people. Decisions are made overwhelmingly by people who do not suffer from, or have any kind of first hand acquaintance with, the affliction they are presuming to fix. Billions of dollars have been devoted to these programs. The evidence of success, based on empirical data that are considered to be the *sine qua non* of social engineering, ranges from unimpressive to counterproductive. If this was really some kind of scientific enterprise, the designers would stop what they are doing and rethink their approaches. Resistance to admitting error is one reason, an understandable reluctance to concede that a promising idea has proved unworkable. Deconcentration does not cure poverty; it does not help most and does harm to many. In several cities, the HOPE VI program had a large impact on real estate, but virtually none of those benefits were shared by the former residents. Access to low-cost housing is even more limited.

Trends in antipoverty programs have continued to favor those that identify and mentor deserving individuals who can be transformed socially and behaviorally into appropriate candidates for ascension into the middle class. Efforts of this kind have negligible effect on the poverty rate or conditions of life for people who are poor, but they are nonetheless very popular. Ruby Payne's system is one part of a larger industry of privatized substitutes for public social services that have been shrinking drastically in the past two decades, and becoming less democratic. In Bridges and Starting Right, Now, and in many other programs that rely on mentors, needful individuals compete to qualify for contingent aid that requires strict adherence to rules and attainment of benchmarked goals. Participants must prove their mettle, showing they have unlearned all the bad habits of poverty culture. To paraphrase Eleanor Leacock from chapter 2, middle-class people want to believe that the poor are truly different from themselves, so they can persuade themselves that it cannot happen to them. More affluent donors and officers of foundations also tend to favor that view of poverty, although their sense of privilege is far less delusional. How do people who are actually poor, those who find themselves dependent on programs of this sort, how do they feel about this rendition of poverty causes and solutions? As Gans pointed out, policy makers have little interest in their feelings, and the voices of poor people are not easily heard.[12] It was not always that way.

We Are All in This Together

An alternative approach to poverty alleviation is collaborative community development, the kind of approach that was envisioned for the CAP programs. The fate of these early efforts to engage poor people in search of solutions to the problems they faced in their neighborhoods was described earlier, and is covered well by Alice O'Connor in her book *Poverty Knowledge*. Moynihan also provided an extended account of these programs, from a highly unsympathetic perspective, in his 1969 book, *Maximum Feasible Misunderstanding*.[13] He rightly condemned some of the provocative and occasionally illegal acts and incidents that littered this brief radical experiment in government-sponsored neighborhood democracy. But his condemnation of the principle—of the idea that poor people have valuable insights and creative energy to offer in finding solutions to the problems they face—revealed much about his own politics.

I began my career in a municipal community development program in the mid-1970s; I later wrote my dissertation based on research I did there on neighborhood social networks and their relationship to the organizational capacities of neighborhoods. My initial job interview took place on the day that President Nixon resigned. I walked through the office door of the Planning Department and saw that people were crowded around a radio on the receptionist's desk. They were listening for news of the resignation, and cheers went up when it arrived. I thought to myself, this could be a good place to work, and it was. It was a heady time, and I was positioned in what turned out to be a very interesting site. The Kansas City Kansas (KCK) Department of Planning, my new employer, was led by a veteran of the CAP wars who remained unbowed in his conviction that good could come from promoting democracy. Part of the backlash against the CAP programs was to reinstate control of federal dollars by local governments. Cities were hence accorded considerable local discretion in implementing the new Community Development Block Grant (CDBG) program. My boss opted to expend a large amount of resources in organizing neighborhood groups throughout the city, whose ideas about their own needs and problems would drive the delivery of eligible services. I was one of three "citizen participation specialists" who served as liaisons between expressed desires and a smooth delivery. At least that was the job description. I also was encouraged and facilitated in my dissertation research about the social dynamics of neighborhoods and evident barriers to the goals of the program. I studied four ethnically and economically diverse neighborhoods, lived in one, went to all their meetings, and interviewed a respectable sample of the residents in all four. I also did participant observation every day at City Hall. After my dissertation research, I undertook a grant-funded study of the history and social networks of a downtown Slavic enclave, a classic urban village named Strawberry Hill, with roots in the early twentieth century when Croatian, Serbian and Slovenian immigrants arrived to work in the packinghouses at the Kansas City railhead. Before I left KCK I had completed another historic preservation study of the very large and spatially concentrated African American community—an utterly fascinating history of African and Native American abolitionist involvement in bleeding Kansas during the Civil War, followed by waves of black migrants who deliberately crossed the free state line and forged a remarkably stable and complex community.

From these research projects, and my earlier intensive involvement in the Community Development Block Grant program, I learned a lot about the neighborhoods of KCK, which were not too different from neighborhoods in most other US cities at that time. I was there long enough (six years, until 1980) to see how difficult it was to organize democratic decision making in neighborhoods, but also how worthwhile. I observed the gradual development of competent and accountable leadership in all four of my neighborhoods, two of which began at the bottom of the scale. One president learned how to do the job and the other was supplanted and replaced by the residents. With really meager budgets, they managed to devise workable plans to address issues they formally agreed were the most urgent. I witnessed some remarkable accomplishments along with a lot of banality that, in the moment, felt like a waste of time. It was no panacea, to be sure, and the program as originally conceived was finally dashed on the rocks of political corruption upstairs from us in the commissioners' chambers. To the extent that this may have turned out to be yet another ineffective abuse-ridden public program, it was not because the people who lived in the targeted neighborhoods had failed in their roles. Indeed, one of the effects later attributed to the neighborhood organizations was a successful movement during the 1980s to restructure city government in KCK, from three white commissioners elected at large, to an expanded multiethnic commission based on district representation with a strong mayor—a large step in the direction of better democracy. There was something organic and reassuring about the neighborhood groups of Kansas City, Kansas. I don't know what has happened to that vision now, and perhaps prefer not to know. What I do recall with pleasure are the many people I got to know there, from a lot of unlikely places and positions, who opened my eyes to the barriers of class and race that had always been before me, but suddenly stood out so clearly.

Collective Efficacy and Neoliberal Visions of Community

Robert Sampson, in a large compendium of his work and thought in and about the city of Chicago, advances the case for making neighborhoods the unit of analysis in inquiries about spatially concentrated disadvantage and related issues like crime and delinquency.[14] In his critique of the MTO design, he argued that focusing on individual outcomes led to results that were confounded by noncompliance and other problems associated with the volition of participants in the study. He implicitly conceded that this approach to concentrated poverty does not seem to have worked. He rejected, however, the notion that poor neighborhoods can be changed through conventional community development approaches, such as the one we tried in KCK. He agreed that neighborhoods of "concentrated disadvantage" often host dense internal social networks and grassroots institutions, like churches and neighborhood organizations, a finding confirmed in my 1970s data. However, he believed these linked structures may be inimical to achievement of what he has labeled the "good community." If networks include gangbangers as well as youthful strivers, or the norms established through these dense connections are hostile to the police and reluctant to take action when witnessing crimes, then the local social structure is deemed incompatible with maintenance of order and cohesion.

Sampson also cites research indicating that strong neighborhood groups may act to exclude certain ethnic groups, indirectly increase the number of hate crimes, and create hostile strongholds. As authority for his skepticism about dense strong ties, he cites the classic article "The strength of weak ties," by Mark Granovetter.[15] Granovetter argued in 1973 that weak ties of acquaintance are more serviceable and valuable than strong ties. The main evidence lay in his contention that job information flows more freely through a ramified network of acquaintances than through the insularity of dense, overlapping ties of kinship and friendship. It is a structural argument that relies on questionable assumptions, including the idea that strong ties entail reciprocal obligations that may be inconvenient for those who are ambitious to rise above their station, i.e., get out of poverty. Another assumption is that dense strong ties are parochial and result in ignorance and blocked access to vital information. Granovetter speculates in his article that the residents of Boston's West End, subject of Herbert Gans's *Urban Villagers*, might have been able to fend off the destruction of their neighborhood by urban renewal if they had been less parochial and had more weak ties to the right people and places. Gans disagrees with this interpretation, and my study of the Strawberry Hill enclave in Kansas City (which also was affected by urban renewal) likewise disputes this assessment. In the latter case, the social ties in the neighborhood were extremely dense, tying together not only the Slavic households but also nearby non-Slavic neighbors. In the 1950s, when the highway was slated to demolish their whole neighborhood, they activated some of those strong ties in City

Hall and other places of influence and managed to negotiate a much less damaging plan that left the Croatian church and a majority of the housing intact.[16] In that setting, strong ties of kinship and shared ethnicity were assets, not liabilities, in the struggle to save their neighborhood. Cohesive networks enabled concerted mobilization. Weak ties would have been less efficacious, less energized. And it is important to note that if the design of the highway could not have been altered to avoid destroying the whole area, then state power would have yielded destruction regardless of the nature of social relationships.

According to Sampson's model, even if people living in poor neighborhoods do have what might be termed "collective efficacy" in a more generic sense, reflected in relatively dense social ties, various kinds of organizations, and in the many inventive ways reported by ethnographers that people have contrived to make life less miserable in contexts of grinding scarcity, it does not count. The critical missing ingredient is a good relationship with the police. Sampson defines collective efficacy as "social cohesion combined with shared expectations for social control." If neighbors are unwilling to call the police when they observe criminal behavior, or if they are willing to tolerate crimes in their families or among their neighbors, then they have failed to meet the criterion for social control. Sampson's blend of cohesion and control envisions a fair and equitable criminal justice system that does not exist.

Police/community relations in low-income minority neighborhoods are typically bad, although some places are worse than others. Reports of antagonism are both widespread and reciprocal, often involving policing that actively provokes and antagonizes. As discussed in chapter 5, abundant reasons explain the lack of trust between "hot spot" residents and police officers. Chicago, Sampson's research site, has been notorious for police violence and discriminatory treatment of African Americans. Take, for example, the case of Police Commander Jon Burge, who oversaw and took part in a regime of tortured false confessions that began in the early 1970s and continued until 2008, when Burge was indicted for perjury and obstruction. The statute of limitations on the torture itself precluded prosecutions on that charge, and in July 2014 a judge ruled that Burge could keep his pension. His egregious and largely unpunished offenses were not committed in isolation, but rather reflected systemic problems. A report released in 2013 by the Department of Political Science at the University of Illinois, Chicago described it as follows:

The case of Lieutenant Jon Burge, Commander of Area 2 Detective Division, accused of torturing suspects to extract confessions is the most notorious, high-profile example of the lack of accountability in the department involving several state's attorneys and mayors. The "blue wall of silence" protected Burge and his many accomplices. Despite numerous courts overturning convictions and several media exposés, the CPD leadership and Mayor's office denied and evaded evidence that Burge and 64 other officers tortured more than 100 African-American suspects over several decades. In addition, dozens, if not hundreds, of police officers, who were present at the stations while the torture occurred or who heard about it from co-workers, failed to report the torture to the proper authorities.[17]

Sampson's insistence on community cooperation with police seems neglectful of realities on the ground, and in interrogation rooms. Over the past decade, Burge's case and other accusations of violent police misconduct have been the focus of periodic media attention in Chicago. Also well known are the lesser but more frequent tensions of stops, frisks, insults, threats, physical abuse, arrests, fines, and expanding criminal records, all too common experiences that weigh against amicable police-community relations. Sampson's quest for a good community surely will have to include a plan for more equitable and respectful policing in so-called disadvantaged neighborhoods.

Securitized Social Engineering

Poverty's abundance offers potential opportunities for private equity to capture public funds and, in the process, redesign antipoverty programs. Billions are being spent on the consequences of poverty, it is argued, but too little goes toward prevention and cure. If innovative prevention and successful treatments for costly problems could be enacted, these measures could save real money. If the savings could be quantified, as in the dollars not spent on each released convict who does not return to incarceration, then investors in preventive programs could be repaid from the resulting tax savings. Investors shoulder the initial risk, offenders get a second chance, society benefits, investors earn a profit, and successful innovation is demonstrated and ready to be scaled up. Everybody wins. At least that is the theory behind a new financial product called "social impact bonds," or

"SIBs," also referred to as "pay for success." These instruments supply funds for innovative, data-driven programs, managed in a businesslike manner, aimed at specified reductions in social ills, and hence avoidance of tax expenditures devoted to remediation. Enlightened finance will invest in social experiments with a high likelihood of success, and apply the genius of the market in preventing and reducing unwanted behavior. What could go wrong?

The Urban Investment house of Goldman Sachs (lately of the securitized mortgage scandal and side bets against their own clients), is in the vanguard of this new sector.[18] In 2012 they joined in a partnership with Bloomberg Philanthropies, the City of New York, and MDRC (a venerable urban policy research outfit) in a $10 million venture designed to reduce recidivism among adolescent offenders at the Rikers Island correctional facility in New York. The program delivers intensive moral education and lessons in how to make better choices (a curriculum labeled ABLE, delivered by another nonprofit, and evaluated by yet another).[19] While this intervention has been underway, however, an unrelated investigation at Rikers Island revealed shocking levels of violence by guards directly, and in failure to protect against attacks from other inmates. Youth offenders have been especially vulnerable to these attacks and they have been disproportionately subjected to solitary confinement.[20] These traumatic conditions would seem to have operated at cross-purposes with the moral lessons conveyed to these same youth by ABLE, or were perhaps just an extra tough love incentive to stay out of the place in future. Whatever the precise impact, such parallel immoral and unrestrained violence surely confounds the expensive cognitive behavior therapy underway.

Such complexities are not within the scope of the investors' agreement. Treatment group recidivism has merely to decline by more than 10 percent below the established control rate in order for Goldman Sachs to recoup its investment.[21] If they fail to reach that threshold, it will be a blow to the budding social impact bonds business. As with earlier ratings of securitized investments, however, measured success for the program might be achievable even under challenging circumstances. Primary control over the evaluation process, and actions at every preceding step, reside with the investor. Public oversight is greatly diminished in this process.[22] Gaming systems is what Wall Street does best.

Concern has been raised that impact bonds may not deliver much impact, but could bleed a lot of public revenue needed for other purposes.

Scarce tax dollars are at stake, along with public control over the nature and quality of social interventions. Lester Salamon points out the SIB product is heavily influenced by investors, who may be among the least qualified to distinguish social programs with a likelihood of success.[23] An exhortation/motivational program aimed at curing moral alienation in youth who were concurrently trapped in a snake pit of violence and corrupt police power seems way short of the task. Investments that might have more direct and positive effects would correct the violent and abusive practices in the facility and reduce the indefensibly large number of juveniles sent there and charged as adults. But those outcomes may be more difficult to monetize, and unlike ABLE, they do not point at the inmates' attitudes as the cause of their own problems.

In spite of what would seem to be obvious pitfalls in the privatization of not only programs, but poverty knowledge itself, social impact bonds, especially the ones that "pay for success," have attracted considerable attention across the political spectrum. This variety of SIB involves a fee for services agreement that pays small sums to low-income clients for performing a set of routine parental responsibilities, like doing annual health checkups and insisting children attend school. Kids get paid for grades and parents get paid extra each week if they work full-time. Experiments in Memphis and the Bronx involve a myriad of rewards designed to instill productive habits and middle-class values. Although the program is intrusive, clients tend to like it because it gives them cash, small infusions that make impossible budgets more workable. Public opinion is strongly against this idea, which is ridiculed as a handout. This disapproval is one reason the pilot programs have relied on private investors. Their involvement brings flexibility in design for all sorts of treatments, and cuts through the cumbersome peer review process for social experiments.

The Center for American Progress, a moderately progressive think tank associated with Democrats, has embraced social impact bonds as a bold new idea that radically reshapes implicitly hidebound public agencies:

> The social impact bond model would also represent a fundamental shift in how service providers are chosen. Today decisions about which providers to fund are typically made by government employees at the local, state, and federal level who review grant proposals and choose providers. With social impact bonds, the private market determines which models and organizations are sufficiently promising to be worthy of financing. The bond issuer and its

service providers will be able to raise operating capital only if private investors are convinced that a program's model and management team are likely to achieve the performance targets. The private investors thus perform an important quality control function.[24]

They do offer words of caution about threats to integrity of measurement and reporting, and the definition of bankable problems, but the possibility of floods of new money coming into social services and evaluation research is apparently seductive.

Turning over "quality control" of social services and programs to the tender mercies of equity traders seems ingenuous at best. Salamon points out that investor-centered projects will not prioritize the interests of low-income clients over those of investors, and points of conflict are not difficult to envision. Similarly, perspectives on measurement and research design inevitably will focus on how to ensure and enhance returns on investment. It also seems likely that preferences for types of services will favor therapy over community organizing, even if the latter might be more likely to succeed. Salamon questions the minimal role of clients in the evaluation process as a threat to the validity of outcome measures. This concern hints also at the absence of clients in other phases of the process, except to absorb lessons, develop constructive habits, and stay out of trouble. What we have now developed is minimum feasible participation.

It is too early to assess the likely impact of financializing poverty reduction. It could be a reach too far to squeeze much money out of already wrung-out public budgets. The trend in policy thinking on both sides of the aisle, however, remains strongly in the direction of individualized efforts to aid the willing and able to rise out of poverty, rather than institutional reforms aimed at structural causes. Investors and philanthropists have tended to support programs like Ruby Payne's Bridges and others that involve mentoring, role modeling, and resocializing members of the dangerous classes. Rep. Paul Ryan's plan for ending poverty envisions a vast system of poverty coaches and outcome recorders who will gather data and apply sophisticated models and algorithms to map choices and achievements, ultimately eliminating the defective values and bad behavior that he believes cause people to be poor. Ryan paid homage to Moynihan in the rollout of his plan, claiming that family structure is the single most important indicator of poverty.[25]

Families do matter. Moynihan was right about that. The people who raise you leave an indelible stamp and shape access to needed opportunities and tutelage. Two parents can earn more income and share parenting tasks, and provide more resources and attention to children than a single mother struggling alone. The presumably optimal condition for social reproduction is the traditional nuclear household. But a growing plurality of families in the United States are not like that for various reasons—some based on choice and many related to economics. More than ten million families are suffering from too much scarcity and debt. The idea that every impoverished family could have a coach to help them develop a multistep plan to escape from poverty is ludicrous on its face, in terms of both the potential costs of staffing such a program and the iron limits of the labor market. Not to mention the extreme level of state intrusion entailed in this suggestion.

We need social policies that allow low-income families to feel and function better, starting with the deliberate dismantling of vicious stereotypes and recognition of the simple facts of social inequality in our nation. Poverty makes family life hard, both for adults and children. As was pointed out by Moynihan's critics a half century ago, a robust correlation between poverty and single parenthood does not mean that the latter caused the former, but it is strong evidence that the two are linked. Much larger societal shifts, of which declining employment for unskilled youth is but one part, have increased barriers to marriage and blocked opportunities for achieving what has been considered normal family life. Instead of engaging in detailed analyses and micromanagement of behavioral and attitudinal responses of youth, single mothers, grandmothers, ex-offenders, or any other target category, it would be useful to involve them from the outset in open-minded bilateral discussions about how to identify solvable problems, improve conditions, and enhance opportunities. I know such an approach can work, and that we really are all in this together.

Notes

Chapter 1 Introduction

1 Daniel Patrick Moynihan, *The Negro Family: The Case for National Action* (Washington, DC: Office of Policy Planning and Research, US Department of Labor, 1965).

2 The term *tangle of pathology* was actually coined by Kenneth Clark, a black psychologist whose work was relied on by the Supreme Court in the 1954 *Brown v. Board of Education* decision striking down "separate but equal." Clark was conducting an applied research project in Harlem, published as "Youth in the Ghetto: A Study of the Consequences of Powerlessness and a Blueprint for Change" (New York: Harlem Youth Opportunity [HARYOU] report, 1964). In a personal communication Herbert Gans suggested that Clark used this term only in passing and not as a significant analytical concept.

3 James T. Patterson, *Freedom Is Not Enough: The Moynihan Report and America's Struggle over Black Family Life from LBJ to Obama* (New York: Basic Books, 2010), 57–58. It is important to note that this so-called finding has been amply refuted by several statistically trained researchers, an issue that will be taken up at greater length in chapter 2.

4 Moynihan, *Negro Family*, 47.

5 Nathan Glazer and Daniel P. Moynihan, *Beyond the Melting Pot: The Negroes, Puerto Ricans, Jews, Italians and Irish of New York City* (Cambridge, MA: MIT Press, 1963).

6 Ibid., 22–23.

7 Other participants were Daniel Bell, Erik H. Erikson, Rashi Fein, Paul Freund, Clifford Geertz, Oscar Handlin, Everett C. Hughes, Carl Kaysen, Edward H. Levi, Jean Mayer, Robert K. Merton, Thomas Pettigrew, Talcott Parsons, Arthur Singer, and William M. Schmidt. Cited in Lee Rainwater and William Yancey, eds., *The Moynihan Report and the Politics of Controversy* (Cambridge, MA: MIT Press, 1967), 22.

Results of this project are published in two issues of *Daedalus*, the official journal of the American Academy of Arts and Sciences (Fall 1965 and Winter 1966).

8 Rainwater and Yancey, eds., *Moynihan Report*, 23.

9 Oscar Lewis, *Five Families: Mexican Case Studies in the Culture of Poverty* (New York: Basic Books, 1959); Oscar Lewis, *The Children of Sanchez* (New York: Random House, 1961); Michael Harrington, *The Other America: Poverty in the United States* (New York: Touchstone, 1962). It should be pointed out that, although Harrington is frequently characterized as an advocate of the culture of poverty argument, his use of the concept differed from Lewis's, and his emphasis was always on the way social inequality and capitalist greed inflicted the misery he was describing.

10 E. Franklin Frazier, *The Negro Family in the United States* (Chicago: University of Chicago Press, 1939); St. Clair Drake and Horace R. Cayton, *Black Metropolis: A Study of Negro Life in a Northern City* (New York: Harper & Row, 1949); W.E.B. Du Bois, *The Philadelphia Negro: A Social Study* (New York: Schocken Books, 1967 [1899]); Kenneth Clark, *Dark Ghetto: Dilemmas of Social Power* (New York: Harper & Row, 1965).

11 Cited in Rainwater and Yancey, *Moynihan Report*, 141.

12 Patterson, *Freedom Is Not Enough*, 71.

13 Reprinted in Rainwater and Yancey, eds., *Moynihan Report*, 375–376.

14 Ibid., 18.

15 Stanley M. Elkins, *Slavery: A Problem in American Institutional and Intellectual Life* (Chicago: University of Chicago Press, 1959). Elkins's work drew strong rebukes from both scholars and activists in the late 1960s and early '70s. See especially Eugene Genovese, "Rebelliousness and Docility in the Negro Slave: A Critique of the Elkins Thesis," *Civil War History* 13 (December 1967): 293–314.

16 Cited in Rainwater and Yancey, eds., *Moynihan Report*, 184–185.

17 William Ryan, *Blaming the Victim* (New York: Pantheon Books, 1971). The *Nation* article, "Savage Discovery: The Moynihan Report" (November 22, 1965) is reprinted in Rainwater and Yancey, eds., *Moynihan Report*, 457–466.

18 James Farmer, "The Controversial Moynihan Report," *New York Amsterdam News*, December 18, 1965, reprinted in Rainwater and Yancey, eds., *Moynihan Report*, 409–411.

19 Geoffrey Hodgson, *The Gentleman from New York: Daniel Patrick Moynihan, a Biography* (New York: Houghton Mifflin, 2000).

20 Alice O'Connor, *Poverty Knowledge: Social Science, Social Policy, and the Poor in Twentieth-Century US History* (Princeton, NJ: Princeton University Press, 2001), 208–209.

21 Rainwater and Yancey, *Moynihan Report*, 176.

22 Carol Stack, *All Our Kin: Strategies for Survival in a Black Community* (New York: Harper & Row, 1974).

23 Herbert Gutman, *The Black Family in Slavery and Freedom: 1750–1925* (New York: Random House, 1976).

24 O'Connor, *Poverty Knowledge*, 208.

25 Hodgson, *Gentleman from New York*, 158.

26 James Q. Wilson and George Kelling, "Broken Windows: The Police and Neighborhood Safety," *Atlantic Monthly* 249 (March 1982): 29–38. This idea, which was widely adopted in cities across the nation, recommended harsh enforcement for

minor offenses, like graffiti and panhandling, to stem criminal trends early. Broken windows policing was warmly embraced by Rudolph Giuliani in New York.

27 The date referred to in this quote is that of the later book, Daniel Patrick Moynihan, *Family and Nation: The Godkin Lectures* (New York: Harcourt Brace Jovanovich, 1986).

28 Even more recently than those references, President Obama's February 2014 announcement of his "My Brother's Keeper" program to resocialize young black men drew numerous comparisons to the message of Moynihan's report. In March 2014 Rep. Paul Ryan, chair of the House Budget Committee, released a report on poverty, which stated that the "single most important cause of poverty is family structure," citing the Moynihan Report as authority.

29 See Michael Katz, *The Undeserving Poor: From the War on Poverty to the War on Welfare* (New York: Pantheon, 1989).

30 Charles Murray, *Losing Ground: American Social Policy, 1950–1980* (New York: Basic Books, 1984).

31 William J. Wilson, *The Truly Disadvantaged: The Inner City, the Underclass, and Public Policy* (Chicago: University of Chicago Press, 1987).

32 O'Connor, *Poverty Knowledge*, 277–283.

33 Michelle Alexander, *The New Jim Crow: Mass Incarceration in the Age of Colorblindness* (New York: New Press, 2010).

Chapter 2 Research and Politics: The Culture of Poverty Knowledge

1 Lee D. Baker, *From Savage to Negro: Anthropology and the Construction of Race, 1896–1954* (Berkeley: University of California Press, 1998), 99–110.

2 Oscar Lewis, *La Vida* (New York: Random House, 1965), xliii.

3 Laura Briggs, "*La Vida*, Moynihan, and Other Libels: Migration, Social Science, and the Making of the Puerto Rican Welfare Queen," *CENTRO Journal* 14, no.1 (2002): 75–101.

4 Douglas Butterworth, "Obituary for Oscar Lewis 1914–1970," *American Anthropologist* 74, no.3 (1972): 751. Butterworth describes a failed effort by board members of the Mexican Society of Geography & Statistics to charge Lewis with "obscenity and slander against the Mexican nation."

5 Oscar Lewis, *Five Families: Mexican Case Studies in the Culture of Poverty* (New York: Basic Books, 1959).

6 Barbara Ehrenreich, "Michael Harrington and the 'Culture of Poverty,'" *The Nation*, March 14, 2012.

7 Carol Stack, "Writing Ethnography against Public Reasoning," keynote address at the Conference on the 25th Anniversary of *All Our Kin* (New Haven, CT: Yale University, 2009).

8 Herbert Gans, in a personal communication, suggested that Moynihan and Harrington were drinking together at the White Horse before Moynihan went to Washington, and likely did not engage in conversations about Oscar Lewis, or other such fancied lines of influence in my scenario. Except for Carol's testimonial, I have no direct knowledge of their mutual influence, but offer it as a metaphor for the convergent, and in some cases opposing, ideas they were formulating in that period.

9   See Herbert Gans, *The War against the Poor* (New York: Basic Books, 1995), 26, where he claims, "Harrington's 'culture of poverty' was an economic term … which paid little attention to 'culture' or its transmission to later generations."

10 Maurice Isserman, "50 Years Later: Poverty and *The Other America*," *Dissent* (Winter 2012).

11 The concept of "subculture" has since gone out of fashion in anthropology, along with the functionalist idea that culture is always adaptive and embraces all of its members equally.

12 Eleanor Leacock, ed., *The Culture of Poverty: A Critique* (New York: Simon & Schuster, 1971).

13 Ibid., 13.

14 Ibid., 18.

15 Charles A. Valentine, *Culture and Poverty* (Chicago: University of Chicago Press, 1968).

16 Elliot Liebow, *Tally's Corner* (Boston: Little, Brown, 1967).

17 Ulf Hannerz, *Soulside: Inquiries into Ghetto Culture and Community* (New York: Columbia University Press, 1969).

18 Carol Stack, *All Our Kin: Strategies for Survival in a Black Community* (New York: Harper & Row, 1974).

19 Valentine, *Culture and Poverty*, 25.

20 Ibid., 29.

21 Ibid., 33.

22 Herbert Gans, "*The Negro Family*: Reflections on the Moynihan Report." 1965 response reprinted in *The Moynihan Report and the Politics of Controversy*, ed. Lee Rainwater and William Yancey (Cambridge, MA: MIT Press, 1967), 450.

23 William Ryan, "Savage Discovery: The Moynihan Report," in Rainwater and Yancey, eds., *The Moynihan Report*, 458.

24 Hylan Lewis, "Agenda Paper #5: The Family: Resources for Change—Planning Sessions for the White House Conference 'To Fulfill These Rights,'" reprinted in Rainwater and Yancey, eds., *The Moynihan Report*, 314–343.

25 Laura Carper, "The Negro Family and the Moynihan Report," reprinted in Rainwater and Yancey, eds., *The Moynihan Report*, 466–474.

26 Daniel Patrick Moynihan, *The Negro Family: The Case for National Action* (Washington, DC: Office of Policy Planning and Research, US Department of Labor, 1965), 47.

27 Alice O'Connor, *Poverty Knowledge: Social Science, Social Policy, and the Poor in Twentieth Century US History* (Princeton, NJ: Princeton University Press, 2001), 205.

28 Carper, "The Negro Family and the Moynihan Report," 469.

29 George Will, "Liberals Can't Wrap Heads around Cultural Causes of Poverty," *New York Post,* March 22, 2014.

30 Daniel Patrick Moynihan, "Families Falling Apart," *Society* (July–August 1990): 21–22.

31 For a very interesting analysis of how the "underclass" concept was born, cultivated, and ushered into a more conservative and punitive view of poverty during the 1980s, see Herbert Gans, *The War Against the Poor: The Underclass and Antipoverty Policy* (New York: Basic Books, 1995).

32 O'Connor, *Poverty Knowledge*, 206.

33 See especially Stephen Steinberg, *Turning Back: The Retreat from Racial Justice in American Thought and Policy* (Boston: Beacon Press, 1995).

34 Carol Stack, *Call to Home: African Americans Reclaim the Rural South* (New York: Basic Books, 1996).

35 Robin D.G. Kelley, *Yo' Mama's Disfunktional! Fighting the Culture Wars in Urban America* (Boston: Beacon Press, 1997).

36 Adolph Reed, ed., *Without Justice for All: The New Liberalism and the Retreat from Racial Equality* (Boulder, CO: Westview Press, 2001). Reed coauthored a seething critique of academics who mounted a petition after Hurricane Katrina, signed by two hundred others, asking HUD to help ensure the permanent dispersal of poor black families from New Orleans. Reed's criticism was highly relevant to the policy known as "deconcentration," explored at length in chapter 4 of this book. Adolph Reed and Stephen Steinberg, "Liberal Bad Faith in the Wake of Hurricane Katrina," *Black Commentator* 182 (May 4, 2006).

37 Sandra Morgen and Jeff Maskovsky, "Perspectives on US Urban Poverty in the Post-Welfare Era," *Annual Review of Anthropology* 32 (2003): 315–338.

38 Brett Williams, *Debt for Sale: A Social History of the Credit Trap* (Philadelphia: University of Pennsylvania Press, 2004).

39 Judith Goode and Jeff Maskovsky, eds., *The New Poverty Studies: The Ethnography of Power, Politics, and Impoverished People in the United States* (New York: NYU Press, 2001).

40 O'Connor, *Poverty Knowledge*, 277–283.

41 Herbert Gans, "The Moynihan Report and Its Aftermaths," *Du Bois Review* 8, no. 2 (2011): 317.

42 Ibid.

43 William J. Wilson, *The Truly Disadvantaged: The Inner City, the Underclass, and Public Policy* (Chicago: University of Chicago Press, 1987), 4.

44 Douglas S. Massey and Robert J. Sampson, "Moynihan Redux: Legacies and Lessons," *The Annals of the American Academy of Political and Social Science* 621, no. 6 (2009): 11.

45 Ibid, 12.

46 See Stephen Steinberg, "Poor Reason: Culture Still Doesn't Explain Poverty," *Boston Review* (January 13, 2011), for another skeptical assessment of this claim that Moynihan's treatment by his critics caused scholarship on poverty and culture to cease for fear of similar scorn.

47 James T. Patterson, *Freedom Is Not Enough: The Moynihan Report and America's Struggle over Black Family Life from LBJ to Obama* (New York: Basic Books, 2010), 71.

48 Elijah Anderson, *A Place on the Corner* (Chicago: University of Chicago Press, 1976).

49 Signithia Fordham and John Ogbu, "Black Students' School Success: Coping with the Burden of 'Acting White,'" *Urban Review* 18 (1986): 176–206.

50 Stanley Lieberson, *A Piece of the Pie: Blacks and White Immigrants since 1880* (Berkeley: University of California Press, 1980); Michael Harrington, *The New American Poverty* (New York: Holt, Rinehart and Winston, 1984); Michael B. Katz, *The Undeserving Poor: From the War on Poverty to the War on Welfare* (New York: Pantheon Books, 1989); Frances F. Piven and Richard A. Cloward, *Regulating the Poor: The Functions of Public Welfare* (New York: Vintage Books, 1993 [1971]); Frances F. Piven and Richard A. Cloward, *Poor People's Movements: How They Succeed,*

How They Fail (New York: Vintage Books, 1979); Edward Banfield, *The Unheavenly City* (Boston: Little, Brown, 1970).

51 Massey and Sampson, "Moynihan Redux," 6–27.

52 Ibid, 9.

53 Rainwater and Yancey, eds., *The Moynihan Report*, 138.

54 W. J. Wilson, "The Moynihan Report and Research on the Black Community," *Annals of the American Academy of Political and Social Science* 621, no. 6 (2009): 39.

55 O'Connor, *Poverty Knowledge*, 205.

Chapter 3   Kinship and Family Structure: Ethnocentric Myopia

1 Daniel P. Moynihan, *The Report on the Negro Family: The Case for National Action* (Washington, DC: Office of Policy Planning and Research, US Department of Labor, 1965), 29.

2 Elizabeth Herzog, "Is there a breakdown in the Negro family?," in *The Moynihan Report and the Politics of Controversy*, ed. Lee Rainwater and William Yancey. (Cambridge, MA: MIT Press, 1967), 344–353. Also see the views of Mary Keyserling of the Women's Bureau of the Labor Dept. and others within government, pp. 178–184.

3 Gregory Acs, Kenneth Braswell, Elaine Sorensen, and Margery Austin Turner, *The Moynihan Report Revisited* (Washington, DC: Urban Institute, 2013).

4 Carol Stack, *All Our Kin: Strategies for Survival in a Black Community* (New York: Harper & Row, 1974).

5 Ibid., 27.

6 Joyce Aschenbrenner, *Lifelines: Black Families in Chicago* (Prospect Heights, IL: Waveland Press, 1975). Smith and Schneider were highly influential anthropological researchers on Caribbean and US kinship.

7 Joye Ladner, *Tomorrow's Tomorrow: The Black Woman* (Garden City, NY: Doubleday, 1971).

8 Nathan Glazer and Daniel P. Moynihan, *Beyond the Melting Pot: The Negroes, Puerto Ricans, Jews, Italians and Irish of New York City* (Cambridge, MA: MIT Press, 1963), 53.

9 Robert B. Hill, *The Strengths of Black Families*, 2nd ed. (New York: University Press of America, 2003 [1972]); Andrew Billingsley, *Children of the Storm: Black Children and American Child Welfare* (New York: Harcourt Brace Jovanovich, 1972).

10 Hill, *The Strengths of Black Families*, vii.

11 Stephanie Coontz, *The Way We Never Were: American Families and the Nostalgia Trap* (New York: Basic Books, 1992).

12 Moynihan, *The Negro Family*, 34.

13 For a very interesting discussion of 1950s psychobabble and suburban housewives, see Brett Williams, "The Great Family Fraud of Postwar America," in *Without Justice for All*, ed. Adolph Reed (Boulder, CO: Westview Press, 1999), 65–89.

14 William J. Wilson, *The Truly Disadvantaged: The Inner City, the Underclass, and Public Policy* (Chicago: University of Chicago Press, 1987), 91.

15 In tribal societies with high male death rates this disparity has been eased by polygyny, or multiple wives.

16 Wilson, *Truly Disadvantaged*, 86.

17 Acs, Braswell, Sorenson, and Turner, *The Moynihan Report Revisited*, 17.

18 D. Madland, K. Walter, and Nick Bunker, "Unions Make the Middle Class: Without Unions, the Middle Class Withers," *Washington: Center for American Progress Action Fund* (April 2011): 519–559.

19 Frank Furstenberg, "If Moynihan Had Only Known: Race, Class, and Family Change in the Late Twentieth Century," *Annals of the American Academy of Political and Social Sciences* 621, no.1 (2009): 94–110.

20 Ibid, 109.

21 See, for example, Steve Macek, *Urban Nightmares: The Media, The Right, and the Moral Panic over the City* (Minneapolis: University of Minnesota Press, 2006).

22 Devah Pager and Diana Karafin, "Bayesian Bigot? Statistical Discrimination, Stereotypes, and Employer Decision Making," *Annals of the American Academy of Political and Social Sciences* 621, no. 1 (2009): 70. Pager and Karafin also present an illuminating discussion of the concept of "statistical racism."

23 Devah Pager, Bruce Western, and Bart Bonikowski, "Discrimination in Low Wage Labor Markets." Working Paper, Office of Population Research, Princeton University, Princeton, NJ, 2007.

24 *The Moynihan Report Revisited* (special issue), *Annals of the American Academy of Political and Social Sciences* 621, no. 1 (2009).

25 Pager and Karafin, "Bayesian Bigot?," 76.

26 Ibid., 90.

27 Harry Holzer, "The Labor Market and Young Black Men: Updating Moynihan's Perspective," *Annals of the American Academy of Political and Social Sciences* 621, no. 1 (2009): 47–69.

28 Ibid., 53.

29 Views of Dr. Benjamin Karney, UCLA professor of psychology, cited by Tom Bartlett, "The Great Mom and Dad Experiment," *Chronicle of Higher Education* (Jan. 20, 2014).

30 Bartlett, "The Great Mom and Dad Experiment."

31 Matthew D. Johnson, "Healthy Marriage Initiatives: On the Need for Empiricism in Policy Implementation," *American Psychologist* 67, no. 4 (2012): 296–308.

32 Ibid., 297.

33 Kathryn Edin and Laura Lein, *Making Ends Meet: How Single Mothers Survive Welfare and Low-Wage Work* (New York: Russell Sage Foundation, 1997); Kathryn Edin and Maria Kefalas, *Promises I Can Keep: Why Poor Women Put Motherhood before Marriage* (Berkeley: University of California Press, 2011); Kathryn Edin and Timothy Nelson, *Doing the Best I Can: Fatherhood in the Inner City* (Berkeley: University of California Press, 2013).

34 Bartlett, in "The Great Mom and Dad Experiment," writes that "Couples who attend all classes receive cash, up to $200, along with points that can be redeemed for baby-related items like diapers, toys, books, strollers."

Chapter 4 There Goes the Neighborhood: Deconcentration and the Destruction of Public Housing

1 Jonathan Salant, "Nixon: Reagan Isn't Pleasant to Be Around," AP, *Boston Globe*, Dec. 11, 2003, http://www.boston.com/news/nation/articles/2003/12/11/nixon _reagan_isnt_pleasant_to_be_around/. The Ehrlichman quote is contained in this story about revelations in the Nixon tapes.

2 The HOPE VI program ended in 2010, replaced in essence by the Choice Neighborhood Initiative and Zones of Promise, which are broader in scope but still permit demolition without one-for-one replacement, a recipe for easy reduction.

3 Edward Goetz, *New Deal Ruins: Race, Economic Justice, and Public Housing Policy* (Ithaca, NY: Cornell University Press, 2013). Goetz provides a sweeping overview of US public housing policy and the variable quality of the complexes. Several were designed by noted architects and were intended to provide wholesome living spaces, part of the progressive New Deal influence. The generalization that all public housing is substandard is too broad. Goetz's evidence also disputes stereotypes about dysfunctional social relationships and norms, even in troubled complexes.

4 HUD overview of Revitalization Programs: "Since the inception of the HOPE VI program, there have been a total of 262 revitalization grants awarded between FYs 1993–2010, totaling approximately $6.2 billion." http://portal.hud.gov/hudportal/HUD?src=/program_offices/public_indian_housing/programs/ph/hope6/grants/revitalization.

5 William J. Wilson, *The Truly Disadvantaged: The Inner City, the Underclass, and Public Policy* (Chicago: University of Chicago Press, 1987).

6 Ibid., p. 8.

7 Charles Murray, *Losing Ground: American Social Policy, 1950–1980* (New York: Basic Books, 1984).

8 The HOPE VI panel study was led by Susan Popkin, director of The Urban Institute's "A Roof over Their Heads" research initiative. Details of the health findings are found at http://www.urban.org/uploadedpdf/311489_hopevi_health.pdf. Other reports are also on that site. Popkin was also one of the principal investigators on the MTO study (along with Xavier de Souza Briggs and John Goering). For a synopsis of findings from the 2008 three-city evaluation of MTO, see Margery Austin Turner and Xavier de Souza Briggs, "Assisted Housing Mobility and the Success of Low-Income Minority Families: Lessons for Policy, Practice, and Future Research: A Three City Study of Moving to Opportunity" (*Metropolitan and Communities Center*, Urban Institute, Washington, DC, Brief #5, March 2008), http://www.urban.org/UploadedPDF/411638_assisted_housing.pdf.

9 Ronald C. Kessler, Greg J. Duncan, Lisa A. Gennetian, Lawrence F. Katz, Jeffrey R. Kling, Nancy A. Sampson, Lisa Sanbonmatsu, Alan M. Zaslavsky, and Jens Ludwig, "Associations of Housing Mobility Interventions for Children in High-poverty Neighborhoods with Subsequent Mental Disorders during Adolescence," *Journal of the American Medical Association* 311, no. 9 (2014): 937–947.

10 Susan Greenbaum, Wendy Hathaway, Cheryl Rodriguez, Ashley Spalding, and Beverly Ward, "Deconcentration and Social Capital: Contradictions of a Poverty Alleviation Policy," *Journal of Poverty* 12, no. 2 (2008): 201–228. See also L. Bennett and A. Reed, "The New Face of Urban Renewal: The Near North End Redevelopment Initiative and the Cabrini-Green Neighborhood," in *Without Justice for All: The New Liberalism and Our Retreat from Racial Equality*, ed. Adoph Reed (Boulder, CO: Westview, 1999), 175–211; Susan Clampet-Lundquist, "Hope or Harm?: Deconcentration and the Welfare of Families in Public Housing" (PhD diss., University of Pennsylvania, 2003), *ProQuest* (AAI3087383), http://repository.upenn.edu/dissertations/AAI3087383; Larry Keating, "Redeveloping Public Housing: Relearning Urban Renewal's Immutable Lessons," *Journal of American Planning Association* 66, no. 4 (2000): 384–397; Goetz, *New Deal Ruins*, 123–155.

11 See John T. Metzger, "Planned Abandonment: The Neighborhood Life-cycle Theory and National Urban Policy," *Housing Policy Debate* 11, no. 1 (2000): 7–40.

12 P. Calthorpe, "HOPE VI and New Urbanism," in *From Hope to Despair: HOPE VI and the New Promise of Public Housing,* ed. Henry Cisneros and L. Engdahl (Washington, DC: Brookings Institution Press, 2010), 49–82.

13 D. Moberg, "No Vacancy: Denial, Fear and the Rumor Mill Waged a War against Moving to Opportunity in Baltimore's Suburbs," *National Housing Institute, Shelterforce Online* 79 (1995), http://www.nhi.org/online/issues/79/novacancy.html.

14 James C. Fraser, A. B. Burns, J. T. Bazuin, and D. A. Oakley, "HOPE VI, Colonization, and the Production of Difference," *Urban Affairs Review* 49, no. 4 (2013): 525–556.

15 W.E.B. Du Bois, *The Philadelphia Negro* (Philadelphia: University of Pennsylvania Press, 1993 [1899]), chapter XV; St. Clair Drake and Horace Cayton, *Black Metropolis: A Study of Negro Life in a Northern City* (Chicago: University of Chicago Press, 1993 [1945]), chapters 19–23; Steven Gregory, "The Changing Significance of Race and Class in an African-American Community," *American Ethnologist* 19, no. 2 (1992): 255–274. See also M. Boyd, "The Downside of Racial Uplift: The Meaning of Gentrification in an African American Neighborhood," *City & Society* 17, no. 2 (2005): 265–288.

16 William J. Wilson and Richard P. Taub, eds., *There Goes the Neighborhood: Racial, Ethnic, and Class Tensions in Four Chicago Neighborhoods and Their Meaning for America* (New York: Alfred A. Knopf, 2006).

17 Robert J. Sampson, *Great American City: Chicago and the Enduring Neighborhood Effect* (Chicago: University of Chicago Press, 2013), chapter 11; Larry Buron, D. K. Levy, and M. Gallagher, "Housing Choice Vouchers: How HOPE VI Families Fared in the Private Market" (Metropolitan Housing and Communities Center, Urban Institute, Washington, DC, Brief #3, 2007).

18 Buron, Levy, and Gallagher, "Housing Choice Vouchers," 5.

19 Tampa's result was slightly higher than the 5 percent found in the Urban Institute panel study. See J. Comey, "HOPE VI'd and On the Move" (Metropolitan Housing and Communities Center, Urban Institute, Washington, DC, Brief #1, 2007), 2.

20 Nan Astone and S. McLanahan, "Family Structure, Residential Mobility, and School Dropout: A Research Note," *Demography* 31, no. 4 (1994): 575–584;. R. C. Fauth, "The Impacts of Neighborhood Poverty Deconcentration Efforts on Low-income Children's and Adolescents' Well-being," *Children, Youth and Environments* 14, no. 1 (2004): 1–55.

21 Sudhir Venkatesh, *American Project: The Rise and Fall of a Modern Ghetto* (Cambridge, MA: Harvard University Press, 2000); Clampet-Lundquist, *"Hope or Harm?";* Lawrence Vale, "Empathological Places: Residents' Ambivalence toward Remaining in Public Housing," *Journal of Planning Education and Research* 16 (1997): 159–175.

22 Sudhir Venkatesh, *American Project;* Alex Kotlowitz, *There Are No Children Here: The Story of Two Boys Growing Up in the Other America* (New York: Anchor Books, 1991). See also Goetz, *New Deal Ruins,* 76–88.

23 Mike Deeson, 10 News Investigators, "Tampa Housing Authority Spent Hundreds of Thousands on Travel," WTSP Channel 10, November 7, 2013, http://www.wtsp.com/rss/article/343415/8/Tampa-Housing-Authority -spent-thousands-on-travel; Deeson, "Federal officials probe Tampa

Housing Authority," Dec 10, 2013, http://highlandscounty.wtsp.com/news/ news/642692-federal-officials-probe-tampa-housing-authority.

24   In January 2014, the HUD investigation was dropped, concluding that THA had not violated any regulations, although the optics were not good. Deeson, "Audit of Tampa Housing Authority: Nothing illegal, but issues are raised," January 24, 2014, http://archive.wtsp.com/news/local/story.aspx?storyid=354142. The Senate investigation continued. Deeson, "Tampa Housing Authority discussed on Senate Floor," January 29, 2014. According to the report, "Senator Charles Grassley is calling the Tampa Housing Authority one of the most egregious for wasteful spending." http://hillsboroughcounty.wtsp.com/news/ news/720232-tampa-housing-authority-discussed-senate-floor.

25   Tom Slater, "Your Life Chances Affect Where You Live: A Critique of the 'Cottage Industry' of Neighborhood Effects Research," *International Journal of Urban & Regional Research* 37, no. 2 (2013): 367–387; Douglas Massey and Nancy Denton, *American Apartheid: Segregation and the Making of the Underclass* (Cambridge, MA: Harvard University Press, 1993).

26   Jens Ludwig, J. R. Kling, L. F. Katz, J. B. Liebman, G. J. Duncan, R. C. Kessler, and L. Sanbonmatsu, "What Can We Learn about Neighborhood Effects from the Moving to Opportunity Experiment," *American Journal of Sociology* 114, no. 1 (2008): 144–188.

27   Susan Clampet-Lundquist and D. S. Massey, "Neighborhood Effects on Economic Self-Sufficiency: A Reconsideration of the Moving to Opportunity Experiment," *American Journal of Sociology* 114, no. 1 (2008): 107–143; R. J. Sampson, "Moving to Inequality: Neighborhood Effects and Experiments Meet Social Structure," *American Journal of Sociology* 114, no. 1 (2008): 189–231.

28   This is a tongue-in-cheek suggestion, but many conservative commentators have opined that foolish borrowing by foolish poor people, abetted by federal fair lending regulations, was the real cause of the mortgage meltdown.

29   Mary Pattillo, *Black Picket Fences: Privilege and Peril Among the Black Middle Class, 2nd ed.* (Chicago: University of Chicago Press, 2013).

30   Mindy Fullilove, *Root Shock: How Tearing Up City Neighborhoods Hurts America, and What We Can Do about It* (New York: Ballantine Books, 2004); David Harvey, "The Right to the City," *International Journal of Urban and Regional Research* 27, no. 4 (December 2003): 939–941; David Imbroscio, "Challenging the Dispersal Consensus in American Low-Income Housing Policy Research," *Journal of Urban Affairs* 30, no. 2 (2008): 111–130.

31   The replacement is actually two programs—Choice Neighborhoods Initiative in Housing and Urban Development, and Neighborhoods of Promise in the Department of Education. The latter is modeled on the Harlem Children's Zone, an ambitious project begun by Geoffrey Canada in about one hundred square blocks of Harlem with tens of millions of dollars in private and public funding. Curing pathology and saving the young are dominant themes. Choice, an outgrowth of HOPE VI, maintains the emphasis on demolition of "distressed" public housing to be replaced by mixed income developments, but is more place-oriented and done in concert with larger redevelopment plans for surrounding neighborhoods.

32   E. Saez, "Striking It Richer: The Evolution of Top Incomes in the United States," 10, http://elsa.berkeley.edu/~saez/saez-UStopincomes-2012.pdf.

Chapter 5   Crime, Criminals, and Tangles of Pathology

1   DrugWarFacts.org, "'Get the Facts,' 53% of state and federal inmates were incarcerated for non-violent offenses in 2012," http://www.drugwarfacts.org/cms/Prisons_and_Drugs#sthash.G2VPUEIv.dpbs.

2   Douglas Blackmon, *Slavery by Another Name: The Re-enslavement of Black Americans from the Civil War to World War II* (New York: Anchor Books, 2008).

3   Michael Lynch, "Reexamining Political Economy and Crime in Explaining the Crime Drop," *Journal of Crime and Justice* 36, no. 2 (2013): 255.

4   Ibid. Lynch notes that "Over that entire time span [1973–2007] the imprisonment rate in the United States has increased each and every year . . . from 96/100,000 population to 506/100,000."

5   Loic Wacquant, "Class, Race, and Hyperincarceration in Revanchist America," *Daedalus* (Summer 2010): 79.

6   Michelle Alexander, *The New Jim Crow: Mass Incarceration in the Age of Colorblindness* (New York: New Press, 2010).

7   Loic Wacquant, *Prisons of Poverty* (Minneapolis: University of Minnesota Press, 2009). Also by Wacquant, *Punishing the Poor* (Durham, NC: Duke University Press, 2009).

8   Wacquant, "Class, Race, and Hyperincarceration," 84.

9   Jeremy Travis, Bruce Western, and Steve Redburn, *The Growth of Incarceration in the United States: Exploring Causes and Consequences* (Washington, DC: National Academies Press, 2014), 107.

10   Many of the harsh sentencing bills were promulgated by the American Legislative Exchange Council (ALEC) as part of a campaign to increase punitive policies and privatize corrections. As of spring 2014, that project appears to have been revised. ALEC is now promoting a bill to end harsh sentences and ease crowding in prisons. Speculation is that they have shifted attention away from the very costly prison-building program to one of expanded privatized parole supervision. Charlotte Silver, "US Criminal Justice System: Turning a Profit on Prison Reform?" *Al Jazeera America*, September 27, 2013, http://m.aljazeera.com/story/201392514144860917.

11   Joe Soss, Richard Fording, and Sanford Schram, *Disciplining the Poor: Neoliberal Paternalism and the Persistent Power of Race* (Chicago: University of Chicago Press, 2011).

12   *Report of the National Advisory Commission on Civil Disorders* (Washington, DC: US Govt. Printing Office, 1968), 93 (also known as the Kerner Commission).

13   These are two cases, both from California, where police brutality followed by exoneration of police stirred unrest in black neighborhoods. Rodney King, who was quoted as saying, "Can we all just get along?" was beaten by police in Los Angeles in 1992, an incident caught on tape that aroused anger in many sectors. Oscar Grant was shot by a transit police officer in Oakland while handcuffed on the platform of the subway in 2009. In Ferguson, Missouri in summer 2014, the killing of an unarmed teenager by a police officer touched off month-long demonstrations and new attention to problems of police-community relations in African American neighborhoods. Also in summer 2014, the chokehold death by police of a black man accused of selling untaxed cigarettes in New York and the subsequent failure to return an indictment in the case sparked nationwide protests involving large crowds in most major cities.

14 Robert Martinson, "What Works? Questions and Answers about Prison Reform," *The Public Interest* 55 (Spring 1974): 22–54.
15 James Q. Wilson, "'What Works?' Revisited: New Findings on Criminal Rehabilitation," *The Public Interest* 61 (Fall 1980): 4.
16 James Q. Wilson and George L. Kelling, "Broken Windows: The Police and Neighborhood Safety," *Atlantic Monthly* (March 1982).
17 Robert J. Sampson and Stephen Raudenbush, "Seeing Disorder: Neighborhood Stigma and the Social Construction of 'Broken Windows,'" *Social Psychology Quarterly* 67, no. 4 (2004): 319–342. The earlier article by Sampson and Raudenbush is "Systematic Social Observation of Public Spaces: A New Look at Disorder in Urban Neighborhoods," *American Journal of Sociology* 105, no. 3 (1999): 603–651.
18 Bernard E. Harcourt and Jens Ludwig, "Reefer Madness: Broken Windows Policing and Misdemeanor Marijuana Arrests in New York City, 1989–2000," *John M. Olin Law & Economics Working Paper No. 317* (University of Chicago Law School, 2006).
19 Ibid., 9.
20 Sherry F. Colb, "A Federal Court Holds New York Stop-and-Frisk Policy Unconstitutional in *Floyd v. City of New York*," *Verdict*, August 21, 2013, http://verdict.justia.com/2013/08/21/a-federal-court-holds-new-york-stop-and-frisk-policy-unconstitutional-in-floyd-v-city-of-new-york#sthash.tX1g1XHY.dpuf.
21 Julia Dahl, "Stop and Frisk: AG's Report Says only 3 percent of NYPD Arrests Using Tactic End in Conviction," CBS News, November 14, 2013, http://www.cbsnews.com/news/stop-and-frisk-ags-report-says-only-3-percent-of-nypd-arrests-using-tactic-end-in-conviction/.
22 *American Civil Liberties Union*, "War on Marijuana in Black and White," June 2013, https://www.aclu.org/sites/default/files/assets/1114413-mj-report-rfs-rel1.pdf.
23 Victor Rios, *Punished: Policing the Lives of Black and Latino Boys* (New York: NYU Press, 2011).
24 US Department of Education Press Office, "Expansive Survey of America's Public Schools Reveals Troubling Racial Disparities," 2014, http://www.ed.gov/news/press-releases/expansive-survey-americas-public-schools-reveals-troubling-racial-disparities.
25 Ibid.
26 Lance Arney, "Resisting Criminalization through ["Obadiah"]: An Engaged Ethnography" (PhD diss., University of South Florida, 2012), Graduate Theses and Dissertations, http://scholarcommons.usf.edu/etd/4278.
27 Ibid., 247–248.
28 Ibid., 249.
29 Blackmon, *Slavery by Another Name*.
30 They can also claw these debt payments from Earned Income Tax Credit refunds and other government-issued checks.
31 K. B. Howell, "Broken Lives from Broken Windows: The Hidden Costs of Aggressive Order-maintenance Policing," *NYU Review of Law and Social Change* 33 (2009): 271–329; Alexes Harris, Heather Evans, and Katherine Beckett, "Drawing Blood from Stones: Legal Debt and Social Inequality in the Contemporary United States," *American Journal of Sociology* 115, no. 6 (2010): 1753–1799; Mary F. Katzenstein and Mitali Nagrecha, "Monetary Sanctions as Misguided Policy: A New Punishment Regime," *Criminology & Public Policy* 10, no. 3 (2011): 555–568.

32 Katzenstein and Nagrecha, "Monetary Sanctions," 557. They cite an average accrued debt of $10,000 for women who are incarcerated. Men serve longer sentences and may have more children. Harris, Evans, and Beckett, "Drawing Blood from Stones," 1777, report an average of $7,234 in LFOs but note that these figures are difficult to assemble and compare for all jurisdictions.

33 Harry Holzer, "The Labor Market and Young Black Men: Updating Moynihan's Perspective," *Annals of the American Academy of Political and Social Sciences* 621, no. 1 (2009).

34 Laureen Snider, "The Sociology of Corporate Crime: An Obituary," *Theoretical Criminology* 4, no. 2 (2000): 169–206.

35 For instance, see Glenn Greenwald, *With Liberty and Justice for Some: How the Law Is Used to Destroy Equality and Protect the Powerful* (New York: Metropolitan Books, 2011); Matt Taibbi, *The Divide: American Injustice in the Age of the Wealth Gap* (New York: Random House, 2014).

36 Michael Kraus and Dacher Keltner, "Social Class Rank, Essentialism, and Punitive Judgment," *Journal of Personality and Social Psychology* 105, no. 2 (2013): 247–261.

37 Paul Piff, Daniel Stancatoa, Stephane Cote, Rodolfo Mendoza-Dentona, and Dacher Keltner, "Higher Social Class Predicts Increased Unethical Behavior," *Proceedings of the National Academy of Sciences* 109, no. 11 (2012): 4086–4091.

38 "Giving and volunteering in the United States," *Independent Sector,* Washington, DC (2002), http://www.independentsector.org/giving_and_volunteering_resources.

39 Angela Pardue, Matthew Robinson, and Bruce Arrigo, "Psychopathy and Corporate Crime: A Preliminary Examination, Part 2," *Journal of Forensic Psychology Practice* 13, no. 2 (2013): 145–169. See also Part 1 of this project by the same authors in *Journal of Forensic Psychology Practice* 13, no. 2 (2002): 116–144; Laurie Ragatz and William Fremouw, "A Critical Examination of Research on the Psychological Profiles of White-collar Criminals," *Journal of Forensic Psychology Practice* 10, no. 5 (2010): 373–402. See also Paul Babiak and Robert Hare, *Snakes in Suits: When Psychopaths Go to Work* (London: Harper, 2007); Belinda Jane Board and Katarina Fritzon, "Disordered Personalities at Work," *Psychology, Crime & Law* 11, no. 1 (2005): 17–32.

40 Paul Babiak, Craig Neumann, and Robert Hare, "Corporate Psychopathy: Talking the Walk," *Behavioral Sciences and the Law* 28 (2010): 174–193.

41 Babiak and Hare, *Snakes in Suits*, vi.

Chapter 6   Commercializing the Culture of Poverty

1 Herbert Gans has labeled it the "Skirmish on Poverty" in *The War Against the Poor: The Underclass and Anti-Poverty Politics* (New York: Basic Books, 1995).

2 Alice O'Connor, *Poverty Knowledge: Social Science, Social Policy, and the Poor in Twentieth Century U.S. History* (Princeton, NJ: Princeton University Press, 2001), 169. On pages 166–173, she provides an excellent account of the struggle over CAP programs in OEO and the pivotal moment in which it occurred. Also, Frances Fox Piven and Richard Cloward, *Regulating the Poor* (New York: Random House, 1993 [1971]), chapter 9, contains a description of this struggle and the politics behind it.

3 Daniel P. Moynihan, *Maximum Feasible Misunderstanding: Community Action in the War on Poverty* (New York: Free Press, 1969).

4   Theresa Funicello, "The Poverty Industry," in *Race, Class, and Gender in the United States: An Integrated Study*, ed. Paula Rothberg (New York: St. Martin's Press, 1992), 121–128. Moynihan was actually a proponent of subsidized allowances for all families with children. This idea was debated during his time as an advisor to President Nixon, but ultimately defeated. O'Connor in *Poverty Knowledge* describes in detail the post-1960s development of research and policy initiatives and institutions that have supported this services-oriented/best practices approach. See also Piven and Cloward, *Regulating the Poor*, chapter 10.

5   Ruby K. Payne, *A Framework for Understanding Poverty*, 4th rev. ed. (Highlands, TX: aha! Process, Inc., 2005 [1996]), 47. The front cover states that she is "the leading US expert on the mindsets of poverty, middle class, and wealth."

6   From blurb on the back cover of Payne, *Framework*.

7   Ibid.

8   Payne's academic critics are many. A few examples of articles by her more active critics are: Nana Osei-Kofi, "Pathologizing the Poor: A Framework for Understanding Ruby Payne's Work," *Equity & Excellence in Education* 38 (2005): 367–375; Jennifer Ng and John Rury, "Poverty and Education: A Critical Analysis of the Ruby Payne Phenomenon," *Teachers College Record* (July 18, 2006); Randy Bomer, Joel Dworin, and Peggy Semingson, "Miseducating Teachers about the Poor: A Critical Analysis of Ruby Payne's Claims," *Teachers College Record* (November 11, 2008); Paul Gorski, "Peddling Poverty for Profit: Elements of Oppression in Ruby Payne's Framework," *Equity and Excellence in Education* 41, no. 1 (2008): 130–148.

9   Payne, *Framework*, 3.

10   Personal communication from Wayne O'Neill to Marilyn Williams on May 29, 2007. Prof. O'Neill studied under Martin Joos. There is lack of agreement about the extent to which poverty, per se, inhibits language development in children, but this instance of Payne's use of Joos's schema is way outside of that legitimate debate.

11   Payne, *Framework*, 3.

12   For example, in Tampa, Florida the daughter of the Title I coordinator for the school district has been lead trainer in the schools. The director of a large CDC (Corporation to Develop Communities) is also a certified Bridges trainer and has brought many Payne events to his center, and there are quite a few other aha! trainers in that city.

13   Philip DeVol, *Bridges to Sustainable Communities: A Systemwide, Cradle-to-Grave Approach to Ending Poverty in America* (Highlands, TX: aha! Process, Inc., 2010). DeVol is Payne's collaborator, and Payne's system is the basis of Bridges.

14   DeVol, *Bridges*, 159.

15   Gorski, "Peddling Poverty for Profit," 141–142.

16   Payne, *Framework*, 12.

17   Paul Gorski, "Savage Unrealities: Classism and Racism Abound in Ruby Payne's Framework," *Intercultural Education* 21, no. 2 (2007): 19.

18   Letter from Ruby K. Payne, PhD, president and CEO aha! Process, Inc. to Mary Ellen Elia, superintendent of Hillsborough County Schools, March 1, 2010. The letter included a fairly detailed account of the meeting written by the man described as her collaborator at the meeting.

19   Gorski, "Peddling Poverty for Profit," 134.

20   Robyn E. Blumner, "The Mind-set of the Poor," *Tampa Bay Times*, Feb. 2, 2013, http://www.tampabay.com/opinon/columns/the-mind-set-of-the-poor/1273.

21 Starting Right, Now website, http://startingrightnow.org/about.html.

22 Peter Jamison, "Tampa Charity Starting Right, Now Sues Homeless Teens it Tried to Help," *Tampa Bay Times*, June 19, 2013, http://www.tampabay.com/news/courts/civil/tampa-charity-sues-homeless-teen-it-tried-to-help.

23 Ibid.

24 Elisabeth Parker, "After Living in her Car, Student Finds a Home and Hope," *Tampa Bay Times*, May 22, 2014, http://www.tampabay.com/news/education/k12/after-living-in-her-car-student-finds-a-home-and-hope.

25 Elisabeth Parker, "Getting Ahead Class Teaches Tampa Woman to Break Habits of Poverty," *Tampa Bay Times*, January 31, 2013, http://www.tampabay.com/news/humaninterest/getting-ahead-class-teaches-Tampa-woman-to-break-habits-of-poverty.

26 Mick Arran, "Poverty and Educational Consultants," *Dispatches from the Trenches* blog, April 17, 2007, http://trenches.wordpress.com/2007/04/17/poverty-and-educational-consultants/.

27 Lisa Delpit, *Other People's Children: Cultural Conflict in the Classroom* (New York: W.W. Norton, 1995).

28 Ward Goodenough, *Cooperation in Change: An Anthropological Approach to Community Development* (New York: Russell Sage Foundation, 1963).

Chapter 7 Ending Poverty as We Know It: And Other Apparently Unreachable Goals

1 Carol Stack, "Writing Ethnography against Public Reasoning," keynote address at the Conference on the Twenty-Fifth Anniversary of *All Our Kin*, Yale University, New Haven, CT, May 2009.

2 Paul Farmer, *Pathologies of Power: Health, Human Services, and the New War on the Poor* (Berkeley: University of California Press, 2003), 8. Johan Galtung's essay is "Violence, Peace, and Peace Research," *Journal of Peace Research* 6, no. 3 (1969): 167–191.

3 Elizabeth Strom and Susan Greenbaum, "Still the 'American Dream'? Views of Home Ownership in the Wake of the Foreclosure Crisis," in *Home: International Perspectives on Culture, Identity, and Belonging*, ed. Margarethe Kusenbach and Krista E. Paulsen, eds. (New York: Peter Lang Academic Research, 2013), 49–72.

4 Stephen Steinberg, *Turning Back: The Retreat from Racial Justice in American Thought and Policy* (Boston: Beacon Press, 1995), 126.

5 Loic Wacquant, *Punishing the Poor* (Durham, NC: Duke University Press. 2009), 51.

6 Daniel P. Moynihan, *Family and Nation: The Godkin Lectures at Harvard University, 2nd ed.* (New York: Harcourt Brace Jovanovich, 1987), 221.

7 Moynihan, *Family and Nation*. On page 228 he states that this collection is a follow-up to Alva Myrdal's 1941 book, *Nation and Family*. Duly noted, but it serves both purposes, and his 1965 report was far better known.

8 This unsourced reference is from *Wikipedia*, which attributes the quote to the work of a lip-reader. Alternative interpretations were that he called him a "kike." Daley's aides objected, saying he actually called him a "faker."

9 Mario Small, David Harding, and Michele Lamont, "Reconsidering Culture and Poverty," *Annals of the American Academy of Political and Social Science* 629, no. 1 (2010): 6.

10 Stephen Steinberg, "Poor Reason: Culture Still Doesn't Explain Poverty," *Boston Review* (January 11, 2011); Herbert Gans, "Against Culture Versus Structure," *Identities: Global Studies in Culture and Power* 19, no. 2 (2012): 125–134.

11 Gans, "Against Culture," 130.

12 An exception is the very popular book by Linda Tirado, *Hand to Mouth: Living in Bootstrap America* (New York: G. P. Putnam's Sons, 2014). The author, a chronically poor mother working several low-wage jobs, wrote a blog about the realities of being poor that "went viral" and resulted in a book deal. In it she recounts her story of the hurdles, indignities, and impossible obstacles of her own and others' lives.

13 Daniel Patrick Moynihan, *Maximum Feasible Misunderstanding: Community Action in the War on Poverty* (New York: Free Press, 1969).

14 Robert Sampson, *Great American City: Chicago and the Enduring Neighborhood Effect* (Chicago: University of Chicago Press, 2012).

15 Mark Granovetter, "The Strength of Weak Ties," *American Journal of Sociology* 78 (1973): 360–380.

16 Susan Greenbaum, "Bridging Ties at the Neighborhood Level," *Social Networks* 4 (1982): 367–384; Herbert Gans, "On Granovetter's Strength of Weak Ties," *American Journal of Sociology* 80, no. 2 (1974): 524–531.

17 John Hagedorn, Bart Kmiecik, Dick Simpson, Thomas J. Gradel, Melissa Mouritsen Zmuda, and David Sterrett, "Crime, Corruption and Cover-ups in the Chicago Police Department," Anti-Corruption Report Number 7, University of Illinois at Chicago Department of Political Science, January 17, 2013, 2–3, http://pols.uic.edu/political-science/chicago-politics/anti-corruption-reports.

18 Richard Teitelbaum, "Secret AIG Document Shows Goldman Sachs Minted Most Toxic CDOs," *Bloomberg News*, February 23, 2010,. http://www.bloomberg.com/apps/news?pid=newsarchive&sid=ax3yON_uNe7I.

19 Timothy Rudd, Elisa Nicoletti, Kristin Misner, and Janae Bonsu, "Financing Promising Evidence-Based Programs: Early Lessons from the New York City Social Impact Bond," MDRC, December 2013, http://www.mdrc.org/sites/default/files/Financing_Promising_Evidence-Based_Programs_ES.pdf.

20 Benjamin Weiser and Michael Schwirtz, "U.S. Inquiry Finds a 'Culture of Violence' Against Teenage Inmates at Rikers Island," *New York Times*, August 4, 2014, http://www.nytimes.com/2014/08/05/nyregion/us-attorneys-office-reveals-civil-rights-investigation-at-rikers-island.html?_r=2#story-continues-2.

21 This goal is not unlikely. The literature on "Moral Reconation Therapy," the approach used in ABLE, does show very modest, but consistent, results in reducing recidivism. L. Myles Ferguson and J. Stephen Wormith, "A Meta-Analysis of Moral Reconation Therapy," *International Journal of Offender Therapy & Comparative Criminology* 57, no. 9 (Sept. 2013): 1076–1106. The critical difference in meeting the 10 percent threshold in the Rikers project is only a few hundred ex-inmates not recidivating over a four-year period.

22 Mildred Warner, "Profiting from Public Value? The Case of Social Impact Bonds," conference paper presented at *Creating Public Value in a Multi-Sector, Shared-Power World*, University of Minnesota, September 2012.

23 Lester M. Salamon, "What Would Google Do? Designing Appropriate Social Impact Measurement Systems," *Community Development Investment Review* 7, no. 2 (2011): 43–46.

24 Jeffrey B. Liebman, "Social Impact Bonds: A Promising New Financing Model

to Accelerate Social Innovation and Improve Government Performance," *Center for American Progress* (February 2011): 12, http://hkssiblab.files.wordpress.com/2012/11/american-progress-report-social-impact-bonds-feb-2011.pdf.

25 Susan Greenbaum, "Debunking the Pathology of Poverty," *Al Jazeera America*, March 26, 2014, http://america.aljazeera.com/opinions/2014/3/culture-of-poverty socialwelfarepaulryanaffluenza.html.

Index

ABLE (moral reconation therapy), 151, 170n21
affluenza, 109, 112
African Americans: criminalization, 61, 66–67, 92–93, 94, 104–106, 113; families, 3, 4, 7, 10–11, 47, 49, 52–57; low income youth, 102–106; marriage, 49; men, 8, 58; neighborhoods, 69, 70–71, 74–75, 77, 101; sharing, 50–51, 53; unemployment, 3, 10, 37, 56–61, 65, 113, 143; women, 8, 9, 160n2
aha! Process, Inc., 67, 117–132; "Bridges out of Poverty," 122, 125, 142, 145, 153; critics of, 168n8; "Getting Ahead," 122, 127, 129, 169n25; marketing, 121–123, 130–132; racial stereotypes, 123–124. *See also* Ruby Payne
Alexander, Michelle: *The New Jim Crow*, 17, 94, 96, 157n33
Alinsky, Saul, 116
American Academy of Arts and Sciences (1964), "The Negro in America," 5–6, 7, 155n7
American Academy of Social and Political Science: *Annals* 2009 Moynihan Revisited, 16, 42, 58; *Annals* 2010 Culture and Poverty, 14; Moynihan Prize, 42
American Legislative Exchange Council (ALEC), 96–97, 138, 165n10

Americans for Prosperity, 137
Anderson, Elijah, 41, 159n48
Arney, Lance, 103–106, 166n26–28
Arran, Mick, 130, 169n26
Aschenbrenner, Joyce, 51, 160n6
Astone, Nan 163n20

Babiak, Paul, 111, 167n40–41
Baker, Lee D., 157n1
Banfield, Edward, 41, 160n50
Bartlett, Tom (Great Mom and Dad Experiment), 161n29
Benedict, Ruth, 20–21
Bennett, Lawrence, 162n10
Billingsley, Andrew, 52
Blackmon, Douglas: *Slavery by Another Name*, 92, 165n2
block-busting, 74–75
Boas, Franz, 20–21
Briggs, Laura, 157n3
Briggs, Xavier de Souza, 162n8
Bronzeville, Chicago, 77
Brookings Institution, 39, 74
Burge, Lt. Jon, 149–150, 170n17
Buron, Larry, 163n17
Bush, Pres. George H. W., 16, 75
Bush, Pres. George W., 75

About the Author

SUSAN GREENBAUM is professor emerita of anthropology at the University of South Florida. For more than three decades, she has been involved in research, teaching, and activism related to poverty, racism, housing, and neighborhoods in the United States. Author of *More Than Black: Afro-Cubans in Tampa* (2002) and numerous academic articles, she is an occasional contributor to *Al Jazeera America* online.

CPSIA information can be obtained at www.ICGtesting.com
Printed in the USA
LVOW07*1041280615

444166LV00001B/1/P